OMNIVM · LVX · CIVIVM

BOSTON
PUBLIC
LIBRARY

D1127056

Narrative Discourse Revisited

GÉRARD GENETTE

Narrative Discourse Revisited

Translated by Jane E. Lewin

Cornell University Press

Ithaca, New York

International Standard Book Number 0-8014-1758-1
Library of Congress Catalog Card Number 88-47730
Printed in the United States of America
Librarians: Library of Congress cataloging information appears on the last page of the book.

The paper in this book is acid-free and meets the guidelines for permanence and durability of the Committee on Production Guidelines for Book Longevity of the Council on Library Resources.

Contents

1 Preamble

As its title surely indicates, this little book is no more than a sort of postscript to *Narrative Discourse*[1]—a postscript prompted, after ten years, by a critical rereading of that "essay in method" in light of the commentaries it gave rise to and, more generally, in light of the advances, or retreats, narratology has registered since then.

The term *narratology* (proposed by Tzvetan Todorov in 1969), together with the "discipline" it designates, has in fact gained a little ground (very little) in France, where nourish-

---

[1][Translator's note.] Ithaca: Cornell University Press, 1980. English translation of "Discours du récit," a portion of *Figures III* by Gérard Genette (Paris: Seuil, 1972). For the present translation, the author modified the original French text in a handful of places. My editorial practices in the present volume have been as follows: (1) Brackets in the text are my interpolation when they enclose a French or English equivalent; specify "in France," "in French," or "in English"; explain something about the French language; or adjust quoted material to its context. All other brackets in the text are Genette's. Brackets in the footnotes are my interpolation when they provide a French equivalent; clarify the relationship between a French text and an English text; explain or identify a reference or comment; adjust quoted material to its context; and give supplementary bibliographical information. Unless otherwise indicated, all other brackets in the notes are Genette's. (2) All ellipsis points are Genette's. (3) When Genette quoted from a work that has appeared in English, the English text has been quoted directly. (4) All translations of French works quoted by Genette are mine unless otherwise noted.

ment of a more aphrodisiac kind is often preferred. It has gained much more ground in other countries, including the United States, the Netherlands, and Israel, as the bibliography at the end of this volume certainly attests.

To some people (including, at times, myself), the success the discipline has achieved is distressing. What irritates them is its "soulless" and sometimes mindless technicalness and its pretension to the role of "pilot science" in literary studies. One could easily counter the mistrust by arguing that, after all, the vast majority of literary (including poetic) texts are in the narrative mode and that it is therefore proper for narrativity to appropriate to itself the lion's share. But I am well aware that a narrative text can be viewed from other angles (for example, thematic, ideological, stylistic). The best, or the worst—in any case, the strongest—justification for the momentary hegemony of narratology seems to me to derive not so much from the importance of the object as from narratology's own degree of maturation and methodological elaboration. A famous scientist asserted in a flash of wit, at the beginning of this century, I believe: "There is physics, then there is chemistry, which is a kind of physics, then there is stamp collecting." No need to specify that Rutherford himself was a physicist, and a British subject. As we know, since then biology too has become a kind of chemistry, and even (if I have read Monod aright) a kind of mechanics. If (I say *if*) every form of knowledge is indeed situated somewhere between the two poles symbolized by rigorous mechanics and that blend of empiricism and speculation represented by philately, we can no doubt observe that literary studies today oscillate between the philately of interpretative criticism and the mechanics of narratology—a mechanics that, I think, has nothing of a general philosophy about it but that at its best is distinguished by a *respect for the mechanisms of the text*. Even so, I am not claiming that the "progress" of poetics will consist of a gradual absorption of the entire field by its mechanical side. All I claim is that the respect in question deserves some respect itself, or some attention, even if only periodically. On leave from narratology (but not from poetics) for more than ten years, I believe I must return to it for a moment, fulfilling the implied promises or threats of my "afterword." And I entreat the potential reader to forgive me the traces of narcissism that such a step will entail. Rereading oneself with an eye on the criticisms incurred is a low-risk activity in which one is constantly at liberty to choose among a triumphant riposte ("I was entirely right"), a not less gratifying apology ("Yes, I was wrong, and I have the grace to admit it"), and a quite self-congratulatory spontaneous self-criticism ("I was wrong, no one else noticed, I am truly the best").

But enough of excuses that are themselves suspect, for self-indulgence has endless subterfuges.[2] Before moving into action, I give notice only that this present account of narrative studies will, for the most part, follow the same order as *Narrative Discourse*: general and preliminary matters (Chapters 1–3), matters of tense (4–6), of mood (7–12), and of voice (13–16), and, finally, subjects not dealt with in *Narrative Discourse* but that today seem to me worth examining, if only to justify rejecting them. Thus, honesty compels me to make explicit what by now has surely become obvious: this book is addressed only to those people who have read *Narrative Discourse*. If you are not among them and have unsuspectingly come this far, you know what it behooves you to do now.

[2]On these subterfuges, see Philippe Lejeune, "Le Pacte autobiographique (bis)," *Actes du IIe colloque international sur l'autobiographie* . . . (Aix-en-Provence: Presses de l'Université de Provence, 1982). Nevertheless, this exercise, which American critics engage in more readily than we do (see the "Second Thoughts Series" of *Novel* [1 (1967–1968)]), may be more conducive in the long run to good health than to bad.

2 Foreword

That title, "Discours du récit," was deliberately ambiguous: discourse about narrative, but also (a study of the) discourse of narrative, the discourse that narrative consists of, a study (as the English translation elected) of *narrative discourse*. It was, moreover, even more ambiguous than I had intended, with that word *discours* hovering between the singular and the plural, at least in the second interpretation. Narrative consists less of *a* discourse than of *some* discourses, two or more, whether one thinks of Bakhtin's dialogism or polylogism or, more technically, of the obvious fact (well emphasized by Lubomir Doležel, and to which I will return) that narrative consists wholly of two discourses (one of which—optional— is, itself, almost always multiple): the narrator's discourse and the characters' discourse(s).

There was another ambiguity, one that the preface fully acknowledged: the duality of object in an undertaking that refused to choose between the "theoretical" (narrative in general) and the critical (the Proustian narrative in the *Recherche*). That duality sprang in part, as all things do, from circumstances. I had formed the intention—if I am not mistaken, during the winter (February to April) of 1969 at New Harbour, Rhode Hampshire,[1] where I was frequently kept at

[1][Geography in the style of Nabokov (see *Pale Fire*).]

"home" by snowdrifts—of testing and systematizing some categories that I had already caught occasional glimpses of,[2] by working on the only text available in "my" house (the three Pléiade volumes of the *Recherche*) and on the random scraps of a literary memory that was already somewhat in distress. A way, like any other—and doomed, indeed, to fail, but I fear that for an instant I had that imp(r)udent pretension—of emulating the manner, the sovereign manner, in which Erich Auerbach, deprived (elsewhere) of a library, one day wrote *Mimesis*. May my colleagues at Harkness University, who are justifiably proud of one of the best literary libraries in the world and who venture out to it in all kinds of weather, forgive me this doubly incongruous parallel, which appears here only for the sake of "the true story."

Whatever the reasons for it, that duality of object troubles me more today than it did then. The systematic recourse to Proustian examples was obviously responsible for certain distortions: an excessive insistence, for example, on matters of time (order, duration, frequency), which take up considerably more than half the book, or too scant a notice of phenomena of mood whose role in the *Recherche* is obviously minor, or even nil (phenomena such as the interior monologue or free indirect discourse). Those drawbacks are undoubtedly offset by certain advantages: no other text could have highlighted, as this one did, the role of the iterative narrative. Besides (is it the specialists' indulgence or their indifference?), the strictly Proustological aspect of that earlier work has hardly been challenged—which will allow me to make a readjustment here and direct the gist of my remarks at matters of a general kind, those that have most engaged the attention of critics.

---

[2]"Frontières du récit," "Vraisemblance et motivation," "Stendhal," "D'un récit baroque," *Figures II* (Paris: Seuil, 1969). [The first and third of those essays have been published as "Frontiers of Narrative" and "Stendhal" in *Figures of Literary Discourse*, trans. Alan Sheridan (New York: Columbia University Press, 1982).]

3 Introduction

I will not return to the distinctions, which today are generally accepted, between *story* (the totality of the narrated events), *narrative* (the discourse, oral or written, that narrates them), and *narrating* (the real or fictive act that produces that discourse—in other words, the very fact of recounting), except to confirm the parallel often drawn between the distinction *story/narrative* [histoire/récit] and the Formalist opposition *story/plot* [fable/sujet]. Confirm it, though, with two faint protests. Terminologically, my pair seems to me more meaningful and more transparent than the Russian pair (or at least than its French translation), whose terms are so inappropriate that I have just hesitated, again as always, over which is which. And conceptually, it seems to me that our full triad gives a better account of the whole of the narrative fact. A two-part division into story and narrative inevitably annuls the distinction between the phenomena that I assign further on to *mood* and to *voice*. Besides, a story/narrative division is very likely to produce a misunderstanding, which is in fact prevalent, between that pair and the pair previously put forward by Benveniste—*story/discourse* [histoire/discours],[1]

[1][Benveniste's English translator rendered "histoire" as "history," but in this context "histoire" has also been rendered as "story" (by John Pier) and as "narrative (or story)" (by Sheridan). See Emile Benveniste, *Problems in General*

which, in the meantime, not wrongly but unfortunately, I had rechristened *narrative/discourse* [récit/discours] to serve another cause.[2]

So *story/discourse, narrative/discourse, story/narrative*—there is plenty here to confuse us unless we are willing to show respect for contexts and let everyone tend his own cows, or count his own sheep, which would certainly make narratology a cure for insomnia. The Benvenistian distinction *story/ discourse*, even or especially if revised to *narrative/discourse*, is irrelevant at this level; the Formalist pair *story/plot* belongs, one may say, to the prehistory of narratology and will no longer be useful to us; as for the pair *story/narrative*, it is meaningless unless incorporated into the triad *story/narrative/ narrating*.

The greatest defect of that triad is its order of presentation, which corresponds to no real or fictive genesis. In a nonfictional (for example, historical) narrative, the actual order is obviously *story* (the completed events), *narrating* (the narrative act of the historian), *narrative* (the product of that act, potentially or virtually capable of surviving it in the form of a written text, a recording, or a human memory). As a matter of fact, only this remanence justifies our regarding narrative as posterior to the narrating. Narrative in its earliest occurrence—oral or even written—is wholly simultaneous with narrating, and the distinction between them is less one of time than of aspect: *narrative* designates the spoken discourse (syntactic and semantic aspect, according to Morris's terms) and *narrating* the situation *within* which it is uttered (pragma-

---

Linguistics, trans. Mary Elizabeth Meek (Coral Gables, Fla.: University of Miami Press, 1971), p. 206; Pier, "Diegesis," in *Encyclopedic Dictionary of Semiotics,* ed. T. A. Sebeok et al. (Berlin: Mouton, 1986); and Sheridan, trans., *Figures of Literary Discourse,* p. 138.]

[2]"Frontiers of Narrative," pp. 137 ff. [See below, Chapter 15.]

tic aspect). In fiction, the real narrative situatio
to—and this pretense, or *simulation* (which
best translation of the Greek *mimésis*), is pr
fines the work of fiction. But the true order is ᴛᴜ

thing like narrating$< \genfrac{}{}{0pt}{}{\text{story}}{\text{narrative,}}$ with the narrative act initi-

ating (inventing) *both* the story and its narrative, which are
then completely indissociable. But has a pure fiction ever
existed? And a pure nonfiction?

The answer in both cases is obviously negative, and the
semiautobiographical text of the *Recherche* illustrates fairly
well the mixture that forms the standard fare of our narratives, literary or not. Nonetheless, the two pure types can be
conceived of; and literary narratology has confined itself a
little too blindly to the study of fictional narrative, as if as a
matter of course every literary narrative would always be
pure fiction. We will return to this question, which at times is
very definitely apposite. For instance, the typically modal
query "How does the author know that?" does not have the
same meaning in fiction as in nonfiction. In nonfiction, the
historian must provide evidence and documents, the auto-
biographer must allege memories or secrets confided. In fiction, the novelist, the storyteller, the epic poet could often
reply, off-fiction, as it were, "I know it because I'm making it
up." I say *off-fiction* as we say *off-mike*, because in his fiction, or
at least in the normal and canonical system of fiction (the one
challenged by *Tristram, Jacques le fataliste,* and a number of
modern narratives), an author is not supposed to be making
up, but reporting. Once again, fiction *consists* of that simulation that Aristotle called *mimésis*.

As for the term *narratology*, its use presents another peculiarity, at least an apparent one. We know that modern narrative analysis began (with Propp) with studies that concerned
the story, considered (as much as possible) in itself and without too much concern for the manner in which it was told—

told or, indeed (for film, comic strip, *roman-photo*,[3] etc.), transmitted by an extranarrative medium (extranarrative if one defines narrative *stricto sensu*, as I do, as a *verbal* transmission). We know also that at present that field is still fully active (see Claude Bremond, the Todorov of the *Grammaire du Décaméron*, Greimas and his school, and many others outside France). Moreover, it is only very recently that the two types of study parted company: "Introduction à l'analyse des récits" by Roland Barthes (1966) and the "Poétique" of Todorov (1968) were still straddling the fence between the two.[4] Apparently, therefore, there is room for two narratologies, one thematic in the broad sense (analysis of the story or the narrative content), the other formal or, rather, modal (analysis of narrative as a mode of "representation" of stories, in contrast to the nonnarrative modes like the dramatic and, no doubt, some others outside literature).

But it turns out that analyses of narrative contents, grammars, logics, and semiotics have hardly, so far, laid claim to the term *narratology*,[5] which thus remains (provisionally?) the property solely of the analysts of narrative mode. This restriction seems to me on the whole legitimate, since the sole specificity of narrative lies in its mode and not its content, which can equally well accommodate itself to a "representation" that is dramatic, graphic, or other. In fact, there are no "narrative contents." There are chains of actions or events amenable to any mode of representation—the story of Oedipus, which Aristotle more or less credited with the same tragic quality in

---

[3][Magazine with love stories told in photographs.]

[4]Seymour Chatman's *Story and Discourse* (Ithaca: Cornell University Press, 1978), Gerald Prince's *Narratology* (The Hague: Mouton, 1982), and Shlomith Rimmon's *Narrative Fiction* (London: Methuen, 1983) have, I would say, gone *back* to straddling it, in the manner of an a posteriori didactic synthesis.

[5]The only claim made to it, so far as I know, is the one set forth by the title (and content) of Prince's book *Narratology* and spelled out in his article "Narrative Analysis and Narratology," *New Literary History* 13 (1982), 179–188.

narrative form as in dramatic form—and we call them "narrative" only because we encounter them in a narrative presentation. This metonymic slippage is understandable but very ill advised. I would therefore readily argue (although without any illusions) for a strict use (that is, one *referring to mode*) not only of the (technical) term *narratology* but also of the word *narrative*, both the noun and the adjective.[6] The way the word has been used has, on the whole, been reasonable until now, but for some time it has been threatened by inflation.

My use of the word *diégèse* [diegesis], partly proposed as an equivalent for *histoire* [story],[7] was not exempt from a misunderstanding that I have since tried to correct.[8] Souriau proposed the term *diégèse* in 1948, contrasting the diegetic [diégétique] universe (the place of the signified) with the *screen*-universe (place of the film-signifier). Used in that sense, *diégèse* is indeed a *universe* rather than a train of events (a story); the *diégèse* is therefore not the story but the universe in which the story takes place—universe in the somewhat

[6]This indicates how disturbed I am by the use of the word as exemplified by a title like *Syntaxe narrative des tragédies de Corneille* (by Thomas Pavel [Paris: Klincksieck, 1976]). To me, the syntax of a tragedy cannot be anything but *dramatic*. But perhaps we should set aside a third level, an intermediate one between the thematic and the modal, for studying what one might call in Hjelmslevian terms the *form of the* (narrative or dramatic) *content:* for example, the distinction (to which I will return in a moment) between what Forster calls *story* (episodic, of an epic or picaresque kind) and *plot* (knit together, of the *Tom Jones* type) plus the techniques belonging to each.

[7]*Narrative Discourse*, p. 27, note. (All further references to *Narrative Discourse* will include only the page number unless the possibility of confusion exists.) "Partly," because a more precise definition appears in [the French index to] "Discours du récit" on page 280. [*Diégétique* is the only term defined in the French index. Its definition is as follows: "As currently used, the diegesis (diégèse) is the spatio-temporal universe designated by the narrative; in our terminology, therefore, in this general sense *diégétique* = 'that which has reference to or belongs to the story'; in a more specific sense, *diégétique* = intradiegetic."]

[8]*Palimpsestes* (Paris: Seuil, 1982), pp. 341–342. Cf. Pier, "Diegesis."

limited (and wholly relative) sense in which we say that Stendhal is not in the same universe as Fabrice. We must not, therefore (as is too often done today), substitute *diégèse* for *histoire*, even if [in France], for an obvious reason, the adjective *diégétique* is being thrust forward little by little as a substitute for the term *historique* [both the adjectival form of the word for "story" and the word meaning "historic"]; that use of *diégétique*, however, would produce an even more burdensome misunderstanding.

Another misunderstanding results from a telescoping of the terms *diégèse*, as we have (re)defined it, and *diégésis*. *Diégésis*, a term we will come upon again, sends us back to the Platonic theory of the modes of representation, where it is contrasted with *mimésis*. *Diégésis* is pure narrative (without dialogue), in contrast to the *mimésis* of dramatic representation and to everything that creeps into narrative along with dialogue, thereby making narrative impure—that is, *mixed*. *Diégésis*, therefore, has nothing to do with *diégèse*; or, if one prefers, *diégèse* (and I had no hand in this) is by no means the French translation of the Greek *diégésis*. Things can get complicated at the level of adjectives (or, alas! of translation: the French and Greek words unfortunately neutralize each other in the single English word *diegesis*, whence such bloopers as Wayne Booth's).[9] For my part, I (like Souriau, of course) always derive *diégétique* from *diégèse*, never from *diégésis*; others, like Mieke Bal, freely contrast *diégétique* with *mimétique*, but I am not answerable for that offense.

The idea of *minimal narrative* presents a problem of definition that is not slight. In writing that "*I walk, Pierre has come* are for me minimal forms of narrative,"[10] I deliberately opted

[9]Wayne C. Booth, *The Rhetoric of Fiction*, 2d ed. (Chicago: University of Chicago Press, 1983), p. 438, note.
[10]Page 30; for suspicious readers, I specify that "Pierre has come" is *not* a summary of Melville's novel, nor "I walk" a summary of *Les Rêveries du promeneur solitaire*.

for a broad definition, and I still do. For me, as soon as there is an action or an event, even a single one, there is a story because there is a transformation, a transition from an earlier state to a later and resultant state. "I walk" implies (and is contrasted to) a state of departure and a state of arrival. That is a whole story, and perhaps for Beckett it would already be too much to narrate or put on stage. But obviously fuller, and therefore narrower, definitions exist. Evelyne Birge-Vitz contrasts my "Marcel becomes a writer" with a definition of story requiring very much more: not only a transformation but also a transformation that is *expected* or *desired*.[11] We may note inverse specifications (a transformation that is feared, as in *Oedipus ends up marrying his mother*), but it is certainly true that the great majority of narratives, popular or classical, require a specified transformation, one that is either gratifying (*Marcel finally, after so many mistakes, becomes the writer he had originally hoped to be*) or disappointing (that is, perhaps gratifying in the second degree, for the reader and, who knows, perhaps even for the hero: *Marcel becomes a plumber*). In any case, to my mind these forms that are specified and therefore already complex are those, let us say, of the *interesting* story. But a story need not be interesting to be a story. Besides, interesting to whom? *I walk* is no doubt interesting only to me—and yet maybe not; or, rather, it depends on the circumstances: after a month in a hospital, it could be a miracle. But, conversely, I know people from whom the specified narrative *Marcel finally becomes a writer* would draw only a lackadaisical "Good for him." It seems to me, therefore, that we must distinguish the degrees of complexity of a story—with or without complications, peripeteia, recognition, and denouement—and leave it to genres, epochs, authors, and publics to

[11]Evelyne Birge-Vitz, "Narrative Analysis of Medieval Texts," *Modern Language Notes* 92 (1977); see *Palimpsestes*, p. 280. As for those who find the summary *more limited* than the work it sums up and who therefore blame a reduction for being reductive, I really have no answer to give them.

choose among them. Aristotle more or less did that and so did E. M. Forster,[12] with his famous distinction between story ("The king died and then the queen died") and plot (". . . of grief"). There are times and places for story; there are times and places for plot. There are even, added Forster, places for mystery: "The queen died, no one knew why." My minimal narrative is undoubtedly even poorer (but poverty is not a vice) than the story according to Forster. Nothing more than "The king died." That, it seems to me, is enough for a headline. And if the crowd wants details, it will have them.

[12]E. M. Forster, *Aspects of the Novel* (New York: Harcourt, Brace & World, 1927), pp. 31 and 82 [rpt. 1954, pp. 15–16 and 52]. Cf. Rimmon, *Narrative Fiction*, pp. 15–19.

4 Order

The study of temporal order opens with a section ("Narrative Time?") that in fact is relevant only to questions of "duration," so I will return to it in that context. Otherwise, the chapter has encountered scarcely more than one criticism, but that one is copious. Bearing solely on the study of analepses (but it would doubtless apply as well, or as badly, to the study of prolepses), it is an article signed C. J. van Rees, published in 1981 in *Poetics* (pp. 49–89), titled "Some Issues in the Study of Conceptions of Literature: A Critique of the Instrumentalist View of Literary Theories."

As the title indicates, the author attacks the "instrumentalist" conception of literary theory. That view, which is supposedly mine, consists of treating theory as an *organon*—that is, an instrument for studying texts. According to van Rees, that view misunderstands the basic principles of methodology in general, illustrates unwittingly and unknowingly a "conception of literature" (that is, a system of norms and values), and serves to institutionalize ideological beliefs about the nature of literary texts. Van Rees invokes a "generative" poetics, one that is convinced of the existence of an innate "poetic competence." The quotation marks are in his text, but I do not know whether he holds me responsible for that phantom and pseudo-Chomskyan idea. For him, in any case, this competence, whose reality, then, he assumes, is in fact *acquired* (I would willingly agree to that, if I knew what it was all about), *heterogeneous* (in other words, I imagine, variable), and *class-bound*, in the Marxist sense of the term. I suppose, therefore, that there is presumably a bourgeois poetic competence, a proletarian one, a feudal one, etc. (Etc.? I have forgotten the official list.) His spelling it out has the merit of pinpointing the origin of instrumentalist criticism and of implicitly (*a contrario*) describing the ideology on which my "conception of literature" is supposedly based: "I shall try to demonstrate by means of a detailed analysis of the first chapter [of *Narrative Discourse*—in fact, of one section of the first chapter, and I leave it to readers to judge the legitimacy of evaluating a 248-page essay by a 19-page sample] why Genette's terminological system pertains to a conception of literature and which are its characteristics" (p. 67). About these "characteristics," the pages that follow are, as a matter of fact, extremely evasive, which does nothing to reassure me: the more diffuse a crime is, the more it deserves hanging, and in matters of ideology, I seem to have hardly any choice, if I have one (and if it is one), except between the bourgeois and the feudal. I hesitate. The only guideline at my disposal—the only reference van Rees assigns to my "conception of literature" (readers will have noted in passing that the mere fact of having one is already serious)—is . . . Wellek and Warren, which is not much help: it is a little late to question them on their own class, which a reading of their work does not sufficiently indicate to me, since I have lost all aptitude for that sort of deciphering. But fortunately, or unfortunately, this dubious ideological assignment is only a preamble to a methodological criticism of the idea of anachrony.

Van Rees sharply reproaches me for my use of the prefix *pseudo-*, linking the term "pseudo-time" that I apply to the duration of the narrative with (in what is more or less his only foray beyond my page 67) the term "pseudo-iterative," which describes certain scenes of the *Recherche*. These two ideas obviously do not have the same epistemological status. The time of the (written) narrative is a "pseudo-time" in the sense that empirically, for the reader, it consists of a space of text that only reading can (re)convert into duration; the pseudo-iterative is *pseudo* in the sense that it is simultaneously presented as iterative (by the use of the imperfect) and unacceptable as such by the manifestly singular nature of its story content (see pp. 121–122, where I call it *license* and *figure* and, more precisely, *hyperbole*,[1] since the author exaggerates the analogy between two comparable scenes into an identity without claiming to be literally believable).

In truth, the iterative itself is always more or less figurative, except when limited to very sketchy statements ("Every day, we took a walk") or very barren contents ("Twenty times a day I wash my hands"). For van Rees (p. 69) there is supposedly a *petitio principii* in speaking of simple resemblance between events presented by the narrative as identical, because the "minimal conditions for resemblance" are not defined. But it is not I who define: it is the text that lays down an identity and I who reduce it by assuming a mere analogy, which that same text reveals to me by pointing out, most often, a whole range of variants (walks in good weather, in cloudy weather, etc.). So let us abandon the attempt to be cautious and let us take the iterative as gospel truth: "Every Saturday, absolutely the same thing happens" (that is what Proust says). That changes absolutely nothing in my definition of the iterative, and it changes even less (if possible) in the fact that the iterative—that is, synthetic—nature of the text is given by Proust, just as, in the classical system (in

---

[1]Catherine Kerbrat-Orecchioni, for her part, defines it as an "aspectual enallage" (an imperfect for a preterite). See "L'Ironie comme trope," *Poétique* 41 (1980), 116; cf. *La Connotation* (Lyons: Presses Universitaires de Lyon, 1977), p. 193. The two attributes are obviously compatible.

Bovary, for example, and still in Proust), the anachronistic nature of an anachrony is *self-declared*. On all these points, my critic is quick to accuse me of being arbitrary. According to him, I decree one or another page to be iterative, analeptic, proleptic, without furnishing *proof*. But I have nothing to furnish: the decree is in the text. True, van Rees does not bother much with the text, and in general his article does not display very much familiarity with the text of, among others, the *Recherche*.

But let us return to analepses, which are all that has drawn his attention. Van Rees accuses me of multiple and incoherent definitions and of basing my terminological propositions on interpretative postulates: I note that he takes a standing leap over my pages 35–48—certainly laborious ones—where I present, starting with examples from the *Iliad*, *Jean Santeuil*, and the *Recherche*, a method for detecting, analyzing, and defining anachronies. The method is no doubt open to criticism, but one cannot say that van Rees has even outlined an examination of it. He is totally unaware of it, as of many other things.

As for the incoherent multiplicity of definitions, I observe further that in order to accuse me of offhandedness apropos of the status of anachronies, van Rees quotes (p. 72) a sentence from *Narrative Discourse* (p. 48; "Discours du récit," p. 90) but purposely omits a word that changes everything: "Ainsi défini," I said, "le statut des anachronies *semble* n'être qu'une question de plus ou de moins, affaire de mesure à chaque fois spécifique, travail de chronométreur sans intérêt théorique." The word omitted by van Rees is *semble*, and it sufficiently indicates that I do not buy that scornful valuation. I know that in fact van Rees is working with the English translation, but here it is perfectly faithful: "The status of anachronies *seems* to be merely a question of more or less, a matter of measurement particular to each occasion, a timekeeper's work lacking theoretical interest." Immediately after, he relies on a more debatable translation of "moments pertinents" (for the discrete distribution of the characteristics of reach and extent) as "certain 'higher' moments in the narrative," on the pretext that the translator perceived the meaning of that passage better than I did: "The translator perhaps comes inadvertently close to the tenor which, for a critical reader, is implied in this passage." One will appreciate the method, free of any "interpretative postulate" and any desire to pick a quarrel.

In the same spirit, eight pages further on (p. 80), van Rees supports his charge of incoherence with a quotation he has heavily doctored. In question is the analepsis, in the *Odyssey*, devoted to the circumstances of Ulysses' wound. I wrote:

> Bien entendu . . . les emboîtements peuvent être plus complexes, et une anachronie peut faire figure de récit premier par rapport à une autre qu'elle supporte, et plus généralement, par rapport à une anachronie, l'ensemble du contexte peut être considéré comme récit premier. Le récit de la blessure d'Ulysse porte sur un épisode bien évidemment antérieur au point de départ temporel du "récit premier" de l'*Odyssée, même si,* selon ce principe, on englobe dans cette notion le récit rétrospectif d'Ulysse chez les Phéaciens, qui remonte jusqu'à la chute de Troie. ("Discours du récit," p. 90)

> Of course, . . . the embeddings can be more complex, and an anachrony can assume the role of first narrative with respect to another that it carries; and more generally, with respect to an anachrony the totality of the context can be taken as first narrative. The narrative of Ulysses' wound deals with an episode that is quite obviously earlier than the temporal point of departure of the "first narrative" of the *Odyssey, even if,* according to this principle, we allow "first narrative" to include the retrospective tale Ulysses tells the Phaeacians, which goes back as far as the fall of Troy. (*Narrative Discourse,* pp. 48–49)

Here again, the English translation is faithful, the "même si" translated as "even if."

This is how van Rees quotes the passage: "First [Genette] states: 'We allow first narrative to include the retrospective tale Ulysses tells the Phaeacians. . . .'" In other words, he quotes a hypothetical-concessive subordinate clause ("even if . . . we allow . . .") as if it were a main clause ("We allow . . ."), thus coolly wiping out the concessive nature of the hypothesis according to which one could, under certain conditions, disregard the analeptic nature of Ulysses' narrative and integrate it into the "first narrative" [récit premier] of the *Odyssey*. Concessive, because here the argument was that *even* in relation to a first narrative beginning at the fall of Troy, the narrative of Ulysses' wound (before the war) remains an external analepsis; what is understood is that a fortiori in relation to a narrative beginning with the departure from Calypso's island, the narrative of the wound is an external analepsis. A three-year-old child would understand this reasoning, but van Rees obviously does not intend to understand.

Such methods condemn a critic. But the basic question raised in all this transcends the person who raises it, or rather, who settles it without having raised it. This question is the relevance and levels of validity of definitions, distinctions, standards, scientific statements in general. Van Rees reproaches me for sometimes disregarding ideas that have been elaborated elsewhere, sometimes neutralizing antitheses set up elsewhere, etc., which for him is a sign of incoherence or even of carelessness. I could claim the right to be careless, but the truth is that intellectual seriousness itself requires one to know how to disregard certain givens. Here I refer the reader to some celebrated pages in *Formation de l'esprit scientifique*[2] about the excess of precision as an epistemological obstacle. At least as much can be said about the excess of rigidity in using categories and definitions, whose value is

[2][By Gaston Bachelard. Published 1938 by Vrin (Paris); currently in its 9th edition (1975).]

never anything but *operative*. At one level of operation, the atom is a system of particles and the earth revolves around the sun; at another level it is better to say, as in the good old days, that the atom is indivisible and the sun rises or sets at a certain hour. At one level of analysis and in relation to the first narrative of the *Odyssey* (that of the epic narrator), Ulysses' narrative to the Phaeacians is an analepsis; at another level, and in relation to a second-degree analepsis, it can be integrated into the first narrative, with the difference between them *disregarded*. Rigidity is the rigor of pedants, who can disregard nothing. But one who overlooks nothing accomplishes nothing.

Otherwise, van Rees's criticism rests on two errors or misinterpretations for which I hold myself a little responsible and which refer us to two weaknesses of my work. His first misinterpretation bears on the study of internal homodiegetic analepses and consists of attributing to me a devaluation, in principle, of all redundancy or interference between the narrative content of those analepses and that of the "first narrative." It is here (pp. 82–85) that van Rees imputes to me a literary aesthetic inspired by the one he attributes to Wellek and Warren, asserting, for example, that "Genette simply assumes that *redundancy* is not present in a good writer." Here, actually, my prejudice, if I have one (I have several), is just the opposite, and on rereading that (too long) chapter on analepses without being at all lenient toward myself, I find that in the chain of distinctions governing it (external/internal, partial/complete, heterodiegetic/homodiegetic), it is entirely constructed with a view to setting off and highlighting the (rare) cases of "risk" of interference and repetition. *Risk* (used twice, pp. 49 and 51) is obviously an unfortunate concession to current aesthetics, which I will not attribute to Wellek and Warren and which requires that repetitions (and contradictions) be avoided. But to my mind, everything nudging Proustian narrative in the direction of interference and repetition was

27

an element of transgression of classical norms and therefore a factor of valorization.

In this area as in others—for example, achronic structures (pp. 79–85), the "game with time" (pp. 155–160), and "poly-modality" (pp. 209–211)—I would be less inclined today to wax enthusiastic, and the attitude that consists of valuing works of the past according to the degree to which they antic-ipate present taste even seems to me a little silly—a puerile avatar of the idea of artistic progress, as if the merit of A were always his heralding of B, who himself was worthless except as a precursor of C, who in turn. . . . Joyce, Nabokov, or Robbe-Grillet have their own value, and Proust has his, and that value is not limited to auguring the value of others.

But even from the viewpoint of a less subjective and anach-ronistic aesthetic than the one occasionally informing *Narrative Discourse*, it is still the case that a narrative's capacities for repetition or "interference" must not be devalued a priori, but very much the reverse.[3] Literature, or at least prose narrative, has always exploited the resources of internal variation much more timidly than have the other arts, particularly music, and has undoubtedly suffered some impoverishment as a result. When a text like the *Recherche* moves in that direction, even unintentionally, one may therefore be permitted to take plea-sure in the fact. At least I never intended to find fault with the *Recherche* for moving in that direction, and I think no one reading my book in good faith could be mistaken in that regard.

The second of van Rees's errors is to (have me) attribute to what I called the "récit premier" [first narrative] a thematic

---

[3]Moreover, I come back to this—and, as one can see, without any modula-tion of a pejorative nature—in the chapter on *frequency* (p. 115), apropos of the repeating narrative of the Robbe-Grillet type. The chief aesthetic merit of this type of narrative, it should be remembered, lies in the way it repeats itself.

preeminence over the anachronistic segments.[4] It ought to be self-evident that I do nothing of the kind, and it seems to me I showed fairly clearly (pp. 43–47) that the most important part of the text of the *Recherche* consists of the vast analepsis that begins with the evocation of the young Marcel's dreams of traveling[5]—the third part of *Swann*. Here too, no doubt, my responsibility lies in clumsy choices of vocabulary, such as "récit *premier*" (passim) or "ligne *principale* de l'histoire" (p. 92) [*main* line of the story (p. 50)]. But still, the latter phrase is directed not at the anachronistic nature of the episodes concerned but, rather, at their *heterodiegetic* nature in relation to what I maintain is (thematically) the main line of the *Recherche*—namely, the hero's experience and apprenticeship. Here I can easily imagine the metacritical obstruction of our Beckmesser[6] ("What *proof* have you that the hero's experience is more important than the marriage of the Cambremer boy?"), but we have already, perhaps, lost enough time. In any case, the term "récit premier" may be felt as connoting a judgment about importance. "Récit *primaire*" would no doubt be more neutral, at least in French, and today I would willingly substitute it. We will encounter its usefulness again, in connection with questions of narrative level.[7]

The problems raised by the study of prolepses are analogous by symmetry, and it is unnecessary to go back over them. By symmetry except, I should say, in importance: nar-

---

[4]Van Rees, pp. 76, 81. The same error appears in Harold Mosher, "The Structuralism of G. Genette," *Poetics* 5 (1976), 81.

[5][Marcel Proust, *A la recherche du temps perdu*, ed. Pierre Clarac and André Ferré, 3 vols. (Paris: La Pléiade, Gallimard, 1954), I, 383; tr. *Remembrance of Things Past*, trans. C. K. Scott Moncrieff and Terence Kilmartin, 3 vols. (New York: Random House, 1981), I, 416. Subsequent references to the *Recherche* will use the abbreviations "P" and "RH" to designate the Pléiade and Random House editions, respectively.]

[6][The town clerk in *Die Meistersinger*.]

[7]"Primaire" is used in this sense by Laurent Danon-Boileau, *Produire le fictif* (Paris: Klincksieck, 1982), p. 37.

rative, even when literary and even when modern, obviously resorts less to anticipation than to retrospection—even if I did exaggerate (p. 36) the canonic nature of the latter technique by attributing an inaugural role to the opening anachrony of the *Iliad* and by contending that "this beginning *in medias res,* followed by an expository return to an earlier period of time, will become one of the formal topoi of epic." Actually, the opening anachrony of the *Iliad* (whose extent, moreover, is very limited) is by no means characteristic of that narrative that, as a whole, is highly chronological; and the formal topos of metadiegetic analepsis is characteristic of the *Odyssey* only—and afterward, by imitation, of the *Aeneid*. Even classical epics like *Jerusalem Delivered* dispense with it, and the chansons de geste hardly think of it. It is by no means a representative feature of epic style in general, and when the phrase *in medias res* itself appears in Horace (*Art of Poetry,* l. 148), it is there not to characterize this Odyssean technique but, rather, to praise the way in which the *Iliad*—without believing itself obliged, even by a completing analepsis, to go all the way back to Leda's egg (*ab ovo gemino*)—thrusts its listeners into the middle of a well-known action (the Trojan War) to take immediate hold of its own subject: the wrath of Achilles. I therefore erred in making an ill-considered generalization, giving too much credit to Huet's view,[8] which elucidates the canon of the Greek and baroque novel more than that of the epic, even the classical epic.[9]

[8]A view that has undoubtedly been fairly prevalent since the Renaissance, for Amyot, introducing his 1547 translation of Heliodorus, asserted, "He begins in the middle of his story, like the heroic poets."

[9]"If one were to label temporally the order of incidents in the *Iliad*, he would discover a perfectly untampered chronology proceeding from the beginning—the quarrel—to the end—Hector's funeral" (Rodney Delasanta, *The Epic Voice* [The Hague: Mouton, 1967], p. 46). Meir Sternberg, who quotes this comment (*Expositional Modes and Temporal Ordering in Fiction* [Baltimore: Johns Hopkins University Press, 1978], p. 37), considers it too unconditional and legitimately rebuts it with analepses like the Catalogue of Ships

To finish up with questions of narrative order, I will say a word about an observation of Dorrit Cohn's.[10] She perceives a "close correlation between Lämmert's temporal conceptualizations and Genette's chapters of Order and Duration." It seems to me that the link thus established between *Narrative Discourse* and *Bauformen des Erzählens* is valid mainly for questions of order—that is, for the study of anachronies. The second part of Lämmert's work is in fact entirely devoted to what he calls *Rückwendungen* (retrospections) and *Vorausdeutungen* (anticipations). I knew the main lines of Lämmert's work when I produced mine, and obviously I ought to have referred to it more. But in spirit the two systems are very different. Lämmert's classification is essentially functional, dividing anachronies according to their traditional position (bound—whether at the beginning or the end—or free) and their role (for analepses: exposition, simultaneity, digression, or delaying; for prolepses: anticipation, whether prescient or not, and advance notice, whether immediate or long range). Despite his apparatus of categories and subdivisions, this long study (92 full pages) is, in a sense, less analytic than mine: it is applied synthetically to canonical forms defined by their position and their function (the titular advance notice, the retrospective exposition, the advance notice as a transition, the epilogue by anticipation, etc.). Our two approaches are therefore complementary. But it seems to me that the order in which they appeared is itself anachronistic and regrettably inverted, with the aesthetic synthesis preceding the textual analysis: Ge-

---

and Nestor's reminiscences. But that does not authorize us to apply to the *Iliad* the formula *in medias res* with its modern meaning, which Sternberg differentiates very clearly from the Horatian meaning (as I do). The temporal structure of the *Iliad* cannot seriously be likened to the temporal structure of the *Odyssey*, which Sternberg, for that matter, analyzes superbly in chapters 3 and 4 of his book.

[10]Dorrit Cohn, "The Encirclement of Narrative," *Poetics Today* 2 (1981), 159, n. 3.

nette is unaware of Lämmert because logically the former precedes the latter, whereas the latter is unaware of the former for a simpler and more compelling reason. Below, another "rearrangement" of the same type will confirm for us that here, as elsewhere, History sometimes goes backward.

5 *Speed*

The difficulty one encounters in measuring the "duration" of a narrative is intrinsic not to the text of that narrative but only to its graphic presentation. An oral narrative, literary or not, has a duration of its own, and that duration is completely measurable. But a written narrative, which in that form obviously has no duration, finds its "reception," and therefore fully exists, only in an act of performance, whether reading or recitation, oral or silent; and that act has indeed its own duration, but one that varies with the circumstances. This is what I called the *pseudo*-temporality of (written) narrative.

Although that difficulty cannot be resolved, it can be *disregarded* if one determines an average or optimal duration of reading—a duration that may be regulated by the text itself, if we are dealing, for example, with a scene of pure dialogue in which the duration of the story is indicated. (In that case, however, what we would be dealing with is only an average regulation, since minor accelerations and decelerations make for a thousand ways of reading one page in three minutes, and no one can say which is the "right" way.) And our difficulty can be all the more disregarded inasmuch as, in this area, the relevant feature is in fact independent of the speed of performance (so many pages *per* hour). The relevant feature is, indeed, another speed, a truly narrative one that is measured by the relationship between the duration of the story and the length of the narrative (so many pages *for* an hour). To compare the two durations (of story and of reading), one must in reality perform two conversions—from duration of story into length of text, then from length of text into duration of reading—and the second has almost no importance except to *verify* the isochrony of a scene. In fact, the isochrony is approximate and *conventional*, and no one (except perhaps van Rees) expects it to be anything else.

So the relevant feature is the speed of the narrative, and for that reason I think today I ought to have entitled that chapter not *Duration* but *Speed*, or perhaps (since, I suppose, no narrative moves forward at an entirely steady pace) *Speeds*. When a narrative itself indicates (or allows one to infer) the temporal limits of its story (not every narrative does), it lends itself easily to a tachometric measurement of the whole. Thus, if (as seems to me the most reasonable course to take) we consider the action of *Eugénie Grandet* as beginning in 1789 and ending in 1833,[1] we can deduce that the narrative covers forty-four years in 172 pages,[2] or about ninety days per page. As for the *Recherche*, it covers forty-seven years in 3,130 pages, or about 5.5 days per page. The three-year-old child who is still by my side thereupon concludes that the *Recherche* is, on the average and *grosso modo*, sixteen times slower than *Eugénie Grandet*, which, as they say, will surprise no one, but who would have guessed it exactly?

I make no claim of great significance for this external comparison; but extending it, as far as possible, to some other major

[1]Pléiade, p. 1030 [trans. Marion Ayton Crawford (Harmondsworth: Penguin, 1955), p. 37]: "Monsieur Grandet . . . was in 1789 a master cooper in a very good way of business"; p. 1199 [Penguin, p. 248]: Eugénie is thirty-seven years old and "lately there has been some talk of a new marriage for her" on the last page, dated *in the text* as September 1833 (which does not necessarily correspond to the real date of writing, which would be irrelevant here).

[2]In the Pléiade edition, to be sure, which I will compare with the Pléiade pages, of the same capacity, for the *Recherche*.

narrative texts might prove interesting. The *internal* comparison consists of measuring, in greater or less detail, a narrative
text's variations of tempo. The measurement performed in
Narrative Discourse for the *Recherche*, however rough it may be
(and however conjectural some of its givens), shows at least
the immense *variability* of Proustian narrative: from a page for
one minute to a page for one century, a relationship that my
three-year-old child announces is 1:50,000,000. A combined
comparison (external + internal) would allow us to establish
a relationship of relationships and, for example, to compare
the Proustian and the Balzacian capacities for acceleration
and deceleration—a comparison that would be highly useful
to a panel of excitement-seekers.

These purely quantitative considerations must be supple-
mented with a more qualitative study, extrapolated from the
classical contrast between summary and scene, to which I
proposed adding ellipsis and pause. Only the latter three
"movements" (in the musical sense) have a given speed: iso-
chronous for scene, nonexistent for pause, infinite for ellipsis. The summary is more variable, but here again we would
need a statistical investigation to measure its variability,
which is perhaps less broad than a priori we imagine it to be.

In reality, the trickiest concept to isolate is the pause. I
define it (p. 94, n. 12) restrictively, in practice reserving the
term for descriptions (and more precisely, for descriptions
taken on by the narrator) when there is a pause in the action
and a suspension of the duration of the story; this, as people
will say without giving the matter much thought, is the Balzacian type. Proustian descriptions (like certain Flaubertian descriptions previously), with their focalized nature, approach
the tempo of scene.[3] That is not the only way to narratize a

[3]Between the two, Zola uses fairly systematically a focalization in theory or
for the sake of appearance that I would readily call *pseudo-focalization*, giving
himself the pretext (thoroughly studied by Philippe Hamon) of a spectator-
character and then, most often, exceeding what would be plausible with that
staging.

description, as we have known since Lessing, whom I invoked by allusion (p. 100, n. 31). But I was wrong to contrast the description of the shield of Achilles with an alleged "descriptive canon" of epic. The Homeric epic, in any case, employs description only rarely; and far from constituting an exception to a Homeric descriptive corpus, the shield could indeed be designated the only object described in detail in Homer.[4] His imitators, such as Virgil and Quintus, dutifully take over from him the topos of the shield, but in them the narratizing precaution (the narrative of the stages of its construction) disappears, and the description therefore constitutes a pause—even if the object described is, in turn, the instrument of a second-degree narrating (a simple animation of the picture as in Quintus, or a real action as in Virgil, where the shield of Aeneas "recounts" the story of his descendants, and notably the battle of Actium), which is indeed narrativity, but a narrativity that is internal to the object described and does not wipe out the pause.[5] It would wipe it out only if the narrator insisted on the perceptual activity of the spectator, and on its duration, which would bring us back to narratization by focalization. There is a little of that in Virgil.

In short, not all description constitutes a pause; but then again, certain pauses are, instead, digressive, extradiegetic, and in the nature of commentary and reflection instead of narration. To deal with something major, let us refer to the essay-chapters that open each book of *Tom Jones* or the histor-

---

[4]The accepted idea that the epic abounds in description undoubtedly comes from the practice of the classical literary theorists, who gave the name "description" to any type of episode that was more or less decorative or diversionary and external to the general flow of the action, like the funeral games.

[5]*Aeneid* VIII; Quintus of Smyrna, *The War at Troy: What Homer Didn't Tell* V [trans. Frederick M. Combellack (Norman: University of Oklahoma Press, 1968)]; cf. Raymonde Debray-Genette, "La Pierre descriptive," *Poétique* 43 (1980), 293–304.

ical-philosophical disquisitions of *War and Peace*. In those cases it cannot be said, as for the descriptive pause, that the narrative slows down by bringing the time of its story to a standstill so as to cast a glance over its diegetic space. Rather, it interrupts itself to give up its place to another type of discourse.[6] One can clearly see, I hope, the difficulty of taking such parentheses into account when measuring the speed of the narrative *in relation to the story*.

In any case, the presence of these parentheses modifies narrative tempo (to prolong improperly the musical metaphor: in the manner more of a fermata than a *rallentendo*); and in a study of tempo, it would perhaps be better to make a place for that fifth type of movement, the reflexive digression. The least one can say is that it is not absent from the *Recherche*. In any case, also, whereas the distinction between the two types of pause may be perfectly clear in principle, in practice and in detail it is often not easy to make. To which of the two types, for example, does this sentence from the *Chartreuse* belong: "Clélia was a little devotee of Liberalism"?[7]

[6]In other words, I see a more pronounced difference between commentarial discourse and narrative discourse than between narrative discourse and descriptive discourse. Or, rather, for me the descriptive (in a narrative) is only an aspect or a modulation of the narrative. I made this point before, but it was not clearly perceived, as we shall see.

[7][Volume 2, chapter 18, trans. C. K. Scott Moncrieff (New York: Liveright Publishing Group, 1925).]

6 Frequency

The chapter on frequency has drawn hardly any criticism, except the incidental one by van Rees mentioned above. Dorrit Cohn, who finds scarcely any original contribution in the first two chapters, very indulgently calls this one "a special (and outstanding) Genettean preserve."[1] Perhaps a little more justice should be done to the study that, in the sequence of critical studies, was crucial: J. P. Houston's. Ten years earlier Houston put his finger on the right spot—that is, on the importance of Proustian iterative.[2] On that subject I have little to add here, except to repeat that Proust by no means invented this type of narrative. Instead, he was the first one (or rather the second, after Flaubert in *Bovary*[3]) to emancipate the iterative from the functional subordination (with respect to

[1]Cohn, "Encirclement of Narrative," p. 159, n. 3.

[2]J. P. Houston, "Temporal Patterns in *A.L.R.T.P.*," *French Studies* 16 (1962), 33–44. The French translation is now in the anthology *Recherche de Proust* (Paris: Seuil, 1980).

[3]Where the iterative has sometimes not been recognized or, indeed, has been misunderstood—a victim of the narrative incompetence of certain readers. Sartre—undoubtedly for lack of knowing how to decode an iterative—seems to have believed all his life that Emma makes love only twice, once with Rodolphe and once with Léon ("Notes sur *Madame Bovary*," *L'Arc* 79 [1980], 40). Undoubtedly Flaubert would have guffawed at the idea of a narrative told coupling by coupling—yet Sartre was not exactly the dumbest of readers. The most *predisposed*, perhaps: he did not need Emma to be *truly* sensual.

the singulative, of course) in which it had been kept by the narrative system of the classical novel. The emancipation amounts even to a complete functional reversal in the form called the pseudo-iterative (in which a manifestly singular event is grammatically converted into the iterative) and in the use of a singular event to illustrate an iterative norm by serving as an example ("Thus, once . . .") or an exception ("Once, however . . .").

Philippe Lejeune points out very correctly that from the time of Rousseau or Chateaubriand, autobiographical narrative has had recourse to the iterative more than fictional narrative has, especially (and very naturally) for evoking childhood memories.[4] The importance of the iterative in Proust is therefore held to result from his imitation of the autobiographical model or from the actual autobiographical element or from both. But we must remember that the iterative is important not only in *Combray* or *Balbec I* but equally in *Un Amour de Swann*, which no longer bears any resemblance to a "childhood memory." Lejeune adds that certain chapters of Book III of *Mémoires d'outre-tombe* (life at Combourg) proceed, like the evocation of Sundays in Combray, by a combination of internal and external diachronies in which are mingled the course of a day, the passage of the seasons, and the aging of the hero. In Chateaubriand the technique, it seems to me, is far less developed than in Proust, but we know how much of his own memory-elicited—and therefore narrative?—system Proust found in Chateaubriand.

In another connection, Danièle Chatelain finds examples of "internal iteration" (*Narrative Discourse*, p. 119) in several scenes from classical novels (Balzac, Flaubert) and even more in Saint-Simon. Here again the affinity is obvious, but we should not—as I did myself apropos of the Guermantes matinée—assign to internal iteration what more simply, and

[4]Philippe Lejeune, *Le Pacte autobiographique* (Paris: Seuil, 1975), p. 114.

more naturally, comes under the heading of the descriptive imperfect. The famous description of the morning sea in the *Jeunes Filles en fleurs* offers, concentrated on two pages,[5] a good opportunity for us to differentiate between these two forms, and also to differentiate between internal iteration ("Every other moment, holding in my hand the stiff starched towel . . .") and external iteration (which in this instance is proleptic): "It was at this window that I was later to take up my position every morning. . . ."

A final word to moderate the formalist bias of the last section of the chapter ("The Game with Time"): the central figure of the Proustian treatment of narrative temporality is undoubtedly what I named *syllepsis*—apropos of the iterative, but we could say as much of the characteristic ordinal structures of, among others, *Combray*, which effect a thematic regrouping of events without regard to their "real" chronological succession (of course, as that sequence is, in the meantime, indicated by the text or inferable from such and such a sign, like the age and pursuits of the hero). Temporal syllepses, therefore; and reminiscence, in its own way, is one of them—one that has been experienced. But metaphor is (in this sense) a syllepsis by analogy, which allows it, as we know, to *represent* reminiscence. In syllepsis, therefore, we might have what Spitzer would have called the Proustian stylistic *etymon*.[6]

---

[5]Proust, *Recherche*, P I, 672–673 [RH I, 723–724].

[6]On p. 115 I evoked the hypothesis of an "anaphoric" narrative, a particular case of the singulative, which would recount a repeating event as many times as the event took place. Shlomith Rimmon (*Narrative Fiction*, p. 57) finds a nice example of that in chapter 20 of *Quixote*, where Sancho undertakes to give a goat-by-goat account of the crossing of the Guadiana, in a boat, by a troop of 300 head. Don Quixote interrupts him in the name of the rights (and responsiblities) of iterative synthesis: "Take it for granted he brought them all across and don't keep going and coming in this way, or you will not finish bringing them over in a year" [Norton Critical Edition, trans. John Ormsby]. Sancho, who has read neither Heraclitus nor van Rees, doesn't think to object that the 300 crossings were not completely identical and loses the thread of his story.

7 Mood

The choice of the term *mood* [French "mode"] to consolidate the questions that pertain to the various techniques for "regulation of narrative information" was convenient and, it seems to me, legitimate, despite the obviously metaphoric nature of the paradigm *tense/mood/voice*. The real disadvantage of the term became clear after the event, when I needed to insist on the truly insurmountable opposition between dramatic representation and narrative,[1] which can hardly be designated otherwise than as the two basic *modes* [French "modes"] of verbal "representation" (those are quotation marks of protest, to which I will return in a moment). Hence the difficulty I have pointed out elsewhere[2] of a single term [in French] for two ideas that are distinct and interlocking, with *mood* ([French] "mode" in the sense in which it was used in "Discours du récit") being one aspect of the functioning of *mode* ([French] "mode" in the sense in which it was used in *Introduction à l'architexte*). Like the woman with the kettle,[3] I

---

[1]*Introduction à l'architexte* (Paris: Seuil, 1979), passim.

[2]*Palimpsestes*, p. 332.

[3][When accused of having made a hole in the kettle she had borrowed, the old woman argued simultaneously that the kettle did not have a hole in it, that it had already had one when she borrowed it, and that the hole she made in it added to its value.]

will plead, first, that I had no choice, since the [French] word ["mode"] is indispensable in both cases; next, that I did well, for it turns out that questions of *mood* ([French] "mode" in the narrow sense) are most characteristic of the narrative *mode* ([French] "mode" in the broad sense), and besides, since narrative is almost always a mixed genre,[4] those questions are exactly the ones in which we see as if *en abyme* the contrast between narrative's purely narrative aspects (*diégésis*) and, with dialogue, its dramatic aspects (*mimésis* in the Platonic sense). Here, therefore, the confusion of terms is highly significant, and in some respects welcome.

I said (again), "regulation of narrative information," although that phrase, with its somewhat overly technical look, sometimes makes people, myself included, gnash their teeth. I will yank out two or three in specifying that I use *information* so as not to use *representation*—a word that, despite its widespread acceptance, seems to me hypocritical, an illegitimate compromise between *information* and *imitation*. Now then, for reasons that have been set forth a thousand times (and not only by me), I believe there is no imitation in narrative because narrative, like everything (or almost everything) in literature, is an act of language. And, therefore, there can be no more imitation in narrative in particular than there is in language in general.[5] Like every verbal act, a narrative can only

---

[4]*Almost* always: this reservation gives me an opportunity to correct a blunder I made in the *Architexte* (p. 28), where I completely excluded the possibility of a long narrative (epic or novel) without dialogue. The possibility is, however, obvious; and Buffon's principle ("everything that may be, is") should encourage one to be prudent; and (barring a new error) there is not a single line of dialogue in *Mémoires d'Hadrien*.

[5]The etymology enthusiast will perhaps find solace in the idea that the Latin *dico* has a family resemblance to the Greek *deiknumi* and, therefore(?), that *to say is to show*. I fear, however, that instead that typifies the incapacity of language from the very beginning to "represent" what it designates unless accompanied by a gesture: *for more certainty, point with your finger at what you are talking about.*

inform—that is, transmit meanings. Narrative does not "represent" a (real or fictive) story, it *recounts* it—that is, it signifies it by means of language—except for the *already verbal* elements of the story (dialogues, monologues). And these, too, it does not imitate—not, certainly, because here it cannot, but simply because it need not, since it can directly reproduce them or, more precisely, transcribe them. There is no place for imitation in narrative, which is always either on one side of it (narrative in the strict sense) or on the other (dialogue). The pair *diégésis/mimésis* is therefore unbalanced, unless we decide, as Plato did, to read *mimésis* as an equivalent of *dialogue*, with the sense not of *imitation* but of transcription, or—the most neutral and, therefore, here the most accurate term—of *quotation*. That is obviously not what the Greek word *mimésis* connotes for us; perhaps (unless we decide to speak our own language) we should replace it with *rhésis*. In a narrative, there are only *rhésis* and *diégésis*—or, as has been said elsewhere, and very clearly, the characters' discourse and the narrator's discourse. That is something like what I was trying to convey with my contrast between "narrative of words" and "narrative of events," but the two sets of contrasts—and I will return to this—are not exact equivalents of each other.

So, despite the clumsiness of the terms, I do not regret thus devaluing the category of *distance*, that is, the quantitative modulation ("how much?") of narrative information—while *perspective*, for its part, governs qualitative modulation ("by what channel?").

8 *Distance?*

My study of modal distance was therefore essentially critical—critical of the old idea of *mimésis* and especially of its modern equivalent, "showing," and therefore of all pairs of oppositions that contain them. But that negative aspect (fairly close to the inspiration behind Wayne Booth's *Rhetoric of Fiction*) was undoubtedly not conveyed clearly enough, since some readers misunderstood it. Mieke Bal, for example, chides me for devoting several pages to a "superfluous" category.[1] I likewise consider it superfluous, but the immense success it has had in various periods made a discussion of it quite necessary, although mine would have profited from greater clarity.

Moreover, it would be a mistake to believe that the valuation inherent in those pairs of oppositions has always worked in the same direction, or in the same way. In the first place, the partisans of mimesis do not always put the same type of narrative stance under that term (or its equivalents). Susan Ringler shows clearly how Lubbock and Chatman, a half-

---

[1]Mieke Bal, *Narratologie* (Paris: Klincksieck, 1977), pp. 26–28. [The first chapter, "Narration et Focalisation" (pp. 19–58), has appeared in English as "The Narrating and the Focalizing: A Theory of the Agents in Narrative," *Style* 17 (1983), 234–269. This particular reference is to pp. 238–240 of "The Narrating and the Focalizing."]

century apart, praise in the name of "showing" two texts as different in manner as *The Ambassadors* and "The Killers,"[2] and today we may wonder at Lubbock's applying the phrase "the story tells itself" to a narrative style as obtrusive as James's.[3] In the second place, those who assign higher value to realism (since, in one way or another, that is always what is at issue) have periodically been counterattacked by those who assign higher value in the opposite direction: Plato against Aristotle (I know); Walzel and Friedemann against Spielhagen; Forster, Tillotson, Booth, against James, Beach,[4] Lubbock, etc. My purpose is not so much to associate myself with this countervaluation (I appreciate Flaubert, James, and Hemingway as much as Fielding, Sterne, and Thomas Mann)[5] as to challenge the very foundation of the debate, or to shift it: once again, the only acceptable equivalence for *diégésis/mimésis* is *narrative/dialogue* (narrative mode/dramatic mode), which absolutely cannot be translated as *telling/show-*

[2]"Chatman designates 'The Killers' as 'showing' because [that text] satisfies his norms for realistic fiction, Lubbock designates *The Ambassadors* because it satisfies *his* norms" (Susan Ringler, "Narrators and Narrative Contexts in Fiction," Ph.D. diss. [Stanford University, 1981], p. 28). Ringler likewise pursues the origin of the pair *telling/showing*, which everyone—either explicitly or, like me (p. 163), implicitly—attributes to the Jamesian school. She shows that in fact it appears neither in James nor in Lubbock or Beach and supposes that it could have been introduced by Welleck and Warren. But we are talking, of course, only about the terms.

[3]Applying it, to be sure, indirectly; in its two most characteristic occurrences (*The Craft of Fiction* [New York: Viking, Compass, 1957], pp. 62 and 113), the phrase is directed at Flaubert and Maupassant. The second occurrence, moreover, is nuanced ("the story *appears* to tell itself"), but the first is much more absolute and plainly normative: "The art of fiction does not begin until the novelist thinks of his story as a matter to be *shown*, to be so exhibited that it will tell itself."

[4]Whose book *The Twentieth-Century Novel: Studies in Technique* (1932) opens with a chapter entitled "Exit Author." To which W. Kayser will answer firmly and accurately (I know): "The death of the narrator is the death of the novel."

[5]To be entirely honest, that isn't true.

Distance?

ing, for "showing" can hardly be applied legitimately to a quotation of words.

The contrast *diégésis/mimésis* leads, therefore, to the distribution into events and words, where it is deflected onto firmer foundations: in the narrative of words, it depends on the degree of literalness in the reproduction of speeches; in the narrative of events, it depends on the degree to which an author has recourse to certain techniques (or, less purposefully, the degree to which certain features are present) that generate the *mimetic illusion*. These features are, it seems to me, the following (perhaps in increasing order of effectiveness):

(1) The supposed obliteration of the narrating instance, which Proust's example, invoked on pages 166–168, at least modifies and perhaps contradicts, and which sends us back to a phenomenon of voice.[6]

(2) The detailed nature of the narrative, and this sends us back to a phenomenon of speed: needless to say, a detailed narrative, in "scene" tempo, gives the reader a greater impression of presence than does a quick and distant summary like the second chapter of *Birotteau*. "On such a multitude of small things," said Diderot, "does the illusion depend."[7]

(3) Finally, and perhaps especially, these details will create even more of an "illusion" if they seem functionally useless: this is the famous "reality effect" of Roland Barthes.[8] Its aesthetic function (for the absence of a pragmatic function[9] re-

[6]Mieke Bal ("The Narrating and the Focalizing," p. 238) implicitly attributes to me the formula "informer + information = C," which I present (p. 166) only to reject it in a free indirect discourse that—I mistakenly believed—was perceptibly ironic.

[7]Denis Diderot, *Eloge de Richardson* (Paris: Garnier), p. 35.

[8]Roland Barthes, "L'Effet de réel," *Communications* 11 (1968), 84–89. [Tr. "The Reality Effect," in Tzvetan Todorov, ed., *French Literary Theory Today: A Reader*, trans. R. Carter (Cambridge: Cambridge University Press, 1982), pp. 11–17.]

[9]By *pragmatic* I mean here (as in *Palimpsestes*) that which relates to the

leases another kind of function) was emphasized by George Orwell in his study of Dickens:

> The outstanding, unmistakable mark of Dickens's writing is the unnecessary detail. . . . The unmistakable Dickens touch, the thing nobody else would have thought of, is [in the story of the little boy who swallowed his sister's necklace in *Pickwick*] the baked shoulder of mutton and potatoes under it. How does this advance the story? The answer is that it doesn't. It is something totally unnecessary, a florid little squiggle on the edge of the page; only, it is by just these squiggles that the special Dickens atmosphere is created. . . . Every time this note is struck, the unity of the novel suffers. Not that it matters very much, because Dickens is obviously a writer whose parts are greater than his wholes.[10]

For his part Michael Riffaterre, apropos of a line by Shakespeare,[11] takes note of these two features, to him fundamental, of a "realistic" line: "First, it is precise [my feature number 2, a detailed narrative]; and in the second place, it depicts an action without indicating the causes or purposes, in such a way that we think we see the thing itself before us."

The agreement among those three writers (I mean Orwell, Barthes, and Riffaterre), who in other respects are entirely different from one another, seems to me an acknowledgment of something obvious—exactly what common sense generally expresses by "That's not made up."[12] But of course the

---

action. According to Propp or the Barthes of "L'Introduction à l'analyse structurale des récits," the functions (par excellence) are pragmatic functions.

[10][George Orwell, "Charles Dickens," reprinted in *Dickens, Dali & Others: Studies in Popular Culture* (New York: Reynal & Hitchcock, 1946), pp. 59–65.]

[11]"And maidens bleach their summer smocks" (*Love's Labour's Lost*, act 5, scene 2); Riffaterre, "L'Illusion référentielle," in *Littérature et réalité* (Paris: Seuil, 1982), p. 102.

[12]Use of these "reality effects" is certainly not limited to literature. Bouvard and Pécuchet read Sir Walter Scott and, "not knowing the originals, they found these pictures convincing, and the illusion was complete" (Flaubert,

pragmatic afunctionality of this kind of detail (the shoulder of mutton in *Pickwick*, or the barometer in "Un Coeur simple," or the shore of the loud-sounding sea in the *Iliad*) can always be challenged by the stalwart upholders of functionalism, who, moreover, take a narrow view of function, since they refuse to acknowledge any function other than a pragmatic one. Thus, Mieke Bal explains that the shore in the *Iliad* has to be loud-sounding *so that* nature, covering up the old man's voice or joining in his prayer, may make common cause with Chryseis . . .[13] Such motivations (for it is one, or I am no judge of these matters) grow out of the same abhorrence of a semantic vacuum, or inability to tolerate contingency, as the wildest (but always facile) Cratylist calculations.[14]

Carried away by her hyperfunctionalist enthusiasm, Mieke Bal even goes so far as to attribute to me "the old prejudice that denies to description any properly narrative function."[15] Aside from the fact that that view, as she herself acknowledges, would be contrary to what I have written elsewhere,[16]

Bouvard et Pécuchet, chapter 5 [trans. T. W. Earp and G. W. Stonier (New York: New Directions, 1954), p. 150]); but Valéry (*Oeuvres*, II, 622) notes in the same way that, in painting, many portraits seem to us to be "true to life" when the model is not (otherwise) known to us: the reason is that they bear signs of realism—such as prominent features, squint-eyes, warts—that no one, or so we think, would invent. At one extreme, to "make true," one only has to make ugly. Inversely, a Virgin by Raphael never seems to us to be a good likeness (of whom?), even though it may just happen to be the faithful portrait of a young Roman woman with perfect features.

[13]Bal, *Narratologie*, p. 93.

[14]It has also been suggested to me that the loud-sounding sea here, as later for Demosthenes, may accompany some speech exercise . . .

[15]Bal, "The Narrating and the Focalizing," p. 239.

[16]*Figures of Literary Discourse*, pp. 133–137. But the phrase *ancilla narrationis* is sometimes interpreted the wrong way, by a curious sliding from ancillary to superfluous. Thus, Lorraine Holmshawi: "[Genette's] theory deprives description of any truly narrative function. Description is accessory, superfluous, aiming at a 'reality effect,' condemned to an ancillary role in narrative" ("Les Exilés de la narratologie," *French Studies in Southern Africa* [1981], 23). More than once, however, the *ancilla* has shown its capacity, if not its aptitude, to become the *serva padrona*.

it seems to me that that conception of the "properly narrative" is terribly narrow: even a description that served only to "make true"—indeed, to "make pretty"—would already be worth something. But in fact I never said any such thing. Let me reiterate: not every description creates a realistic effect; and reciprocally, not every realistic effect is necessarily descriptive—for example, "He blew his nose noisily and said, . . ." or the Shakespearean line quoted by Riffaterre. A detail that is "unnecessary for the action" may very well be, in itself, an action.

A more serious objection would seem to me to be this one: *at the time* (that is, on a first reading), nothing tells us whether a detail will or will not turn out to have a pragmatic function—some day Mme Aubain's barometer could fall on Virginie and kill her.[17] Its role as an agent of mimesis can therefore emerge only *retroactively*, on a second reading or a subsequent recalling, which is not very compatible with the effect of immediacy it is supposed to be aiming for. This objection is not stupid (and for good reason), but it also seems to me that a certain competence with narrative style can help the reader intuitively perceive the pragmatic or nonpragmatic nature of one or another detail. There is a code in this, and of course "one knows" that a barometer, or even a pistol, can hardly have the same function in Flaubert as in Agatha Christie.

---

[17]"[According to Chekhov], if one speaks about a nail beaten into a wall at the beginning of a narrative, then at the end the hero must hang himself on that nail" (Boris Tomashevsky, "Thematics," in *Russian Formalist Criticism: Four Essays* [Lincoln: University of Nebraska Press, 1965], p. 79).

9 *Narrative of Words*

The section devoted to "narrative of words" (pp. 169–185) could usefully be retitled "Modes of (Re)Production of the Speech and Thought of Characters in Written Literary Narrative." *(Re)production* would indicate the fictive or nonfictive nature of the model, depending on the genre: history, biography, autobiography are supposed to reproduce speeches that were actually made; epic, novel, story, novella are supposed to pretend to reproduce them and therefore in reality are supposed to *produce* speeches invented from whole cloth. *Supposed to*: those are the generic conventions, which of course do not necessarily correspond to reality. Livy can invent a harangue, Proust can attribute to one of his heroes some sentence actually spoken to his face (or behind his back) by some real person. If we agree to disregard these transgressions, the production of speech proper to fiction is a fictive reproduction, based fictively on the same contracts, and presenting fictively the same difficulties, as genuine reproduction. The same contracts: for example, quotation marks indicate (promise) a literal quotation, a subordinate clause in indirect style allows more freedom, etc. The same difficulties: literal (re)production may (be supposed to) have undergone translation, like the speeches of the Roman leaders in Polybius or Plutarch or those of the heroes of *La Chartreuse* or

L'Espoir, which somewhat undermines its literalness—and in all cases the "passage" from the spoken to the written almost irremediably neutralizes the particularities of expression: timbre, intonation, accent, etc. *Almost*: the novelist or historian can have recourse to palliatives that are either external (description of timbre and intonation) or internal (phonetic notations, as in Balzac, Dickens, or Proust). The term *(re)production* itself should therefore not be taken too literally—and certain of its limitations would apply even to the oral forms of narrative. No storyteller, for example, can reproduce absolutely the vocal quality of every one of his characters. The contract of literalness never applies to anything except the actual *content* of speech.

These restrictions, I repeat, affect only one of the modes of (re)production, the one I have called "reported speech." The two others ("transposed" and "narratized" speech) officially fall very far short of such a problematic, since they do not aim for the same "mimeticism"—that is, the same literalness. This tripartite division—which is common, moreover, except for the terms—has not in itself been challenged, but some aspects of it have been criticized by Dorrit Cohn.[1]

If we set aside a purely terminological disagreement to which I will return, Dorrit Cohn has three main criticisms. The first is that I did not sufficiently develop the study of what I called "immediate speech" and what she quite properly proposes to christen instead *autonomous monologue*: we are dealing here with the type of speech that, since Dujardin, has traditionally been called "interior monologue." This criticism obviously makes sense: I devote barely two pages to the form (pp. 173–175). The reason, as I have already said, is the rarity of the technique in Proust. But I am readily consoled for my oversight by the excellent sixth chapter of *Transparent*

[1]Dorrit Cohn, *Transparent Minds* (Princeton: Princeton University Press, 1978) and "Encirclement of Narrative."

Minds, which fills the gap better than I ever could have. All I need do, therefore, is refer the reader to it.

The second deficiency pointed out and remedied by Dorrit Cohn: the too-brief paragraph that *Narrative Discourse* devoted (p. 172) to "free indirect style." I presented it as a simple "variant" of indirect style and limited myself to pointing out, as others had done, the double ambiguity involved: confusion between speech and thought, between character and narrator. Here again, the main reason for my circumspection was the relative rarity of this form in Proust. Another reason will, today, make the specialists smile: it seemed to me that since its "discovery" at the turn of the century, the subject had been sufficiently treated from the grammatical and stylistic point of view (my one and only reference was the book by Marguerite Lips, which still seems to me the most satisfactory contribution of the Geneva School). Since 1972, the bibliography on the subject has been considerably augmented—for example, by Roy Pascal's book[2] and Dorrit Cohn's chapter 3, and by a substantial controversy stirred up by an article of Ann Banfield's.[3] Here I have no reason to go back over that long story, which is probably not closed and in which several linguistic schools (Vosslerian psychologism, Saussurian structuralism, Bakhtinian neo-Hegelianism, and various trends in transformational grammar)—schools among which I do not care to arbitrate—have become active and clashed over a stylistic-grammatical form. The highly selective bibliography of this opuscule contains a good twenty titles relating to it, and for an (almost) up-to-date approach to the issue I refer readers to the clarification by Brian McHale.[4]

[2]Roy Pascal, *The Dual Voice: Free Indirect Speech and Its Functioning in the Nineteenth Century European Novel* (Manchester: Manchester University Press, 1977).

[3]Ann Banfield, "Narrative Style and the Grammar of Direct and Indirect Speech, *Foundations of Language* 10 (1973).

[4]Brian McHale, "Free Indirect Discourse: A Survey of Recent Accounts," *PTL* 3:2 (April 1978).

To put in my own two cents' worth, I shall add just a few remarks here. Regarding the strictly grammatical description of the phenomenon: it seems to me that, on this point as on some others, transformational grammar has provided only a methodological congestion ill justified by its actual contribution; that the essentials (agreement of tenses, conversion of pronouns, absence of grammatical government, maintenance of the deictics of proximity, of direct interrogation, of certain interjective and expressive features) have been established since the time of Bally and Lips; and that the consensus, except in ways of proceeding, is very broad. Agreement of tenses, however, is probably not a hard and fast rule (if, indeed, there is one in a type so open to stylistic initiative). The expression of an opinion that derives, or is thought to derive, from scholarship or from an atemporal verity can involve a transition to the gnomic, or epistemic, present. Thus, in *Bouvard et Pécuchet:* "They even wished to learn Hebrew, which *is* the mother-language of Celtic, unless it *is* derived from it," or "Administrative justice was a monstrosity, for the administration *governs* its servants unjustly by threats and favours."[5] Marie-Thérèse Jacquet, from whom I take these examples, has clearly highlighted the importance of this form in *Bouvard*. But her term *integrated direct style* seems to me to draw this intermediary form too much in the direction of direct style; I would prefer to keep this form in the realm of free indirect speech, using a phrase such as "free indirect speech without agreement of tenses." The investigation of this device should be expanded. Flaubert undoubtedly does not have a monopoly on it, even if the encyclopedicomaniac context of *Bouvard* particularly lends itself to its use.

Regarding the stylistic distribution: despite some nuances and exceptions as marginal as they are obvious, the basically literary nature of the technique seems to me indisputable. Ann Banfield extends this feature as far as to make the free

[5][Trans. Earp and Stonier, chapter 4, p. 131, and chapter 10, p. 338.]

indirect the sign of a noncommunicative mode of language, to the exclusion of the first and especially the second person,[6] giving short shrift to the free indirect's indisputable presence in autodiegetic narrating. A (famous) example in Dickens: "My dream was out; my wild fancy was surpassed by sober reality; Miss Havisham was going to make my fortune on a grand scale"[7]—the follow-up to which shows very vividly that those thoughts were the hero's (mistaken) thoughts, not the narrator's. Another example, in Balzac, this time from the mouth of a character who is reporting her own earlier speech: "I had said such touching things to him; that I was jealous by nature and an infidelity would kill me. . . ."[8]

Regarding the historical distribution: here again, with some exceptions (La Fontaine, Rousseau), it corresponds very clearly to the era of the psycho-realistic "modern" novel, from Jane Austen to Thomas Mann, and more precisely to the narrative mode I call "internal focalization," one of whose favorite instruments is definitely free indirect style. Happily, I was not the first to note it: Franz Stanzel did so in 1955, although the terms he used were different.

That comment obviously opens onto another aspect, for us the main one, which is the narrative function of free indirect style. A strong case has been made (earlier by the Vosslerians; nowadays by Cohn, Pascal, Banfield) that this "style" is fundamentally better suited to expressing innermost thoughts

---

[6]In her recent book (*Unspeakable Sentences: Narration and Representation in the Language of Fiction* [Boston and London: Routledge & Kegan Paul, 1982]), Banfield upholds against all objections, and emphasizes to the point of caricature, an even more extreme argument according to which the free indirect style—a form that is alien and even, according to her, impossible in the spoken language ("unspeakable")—reveals, as do statements in the aorist (which are also unspeakable), an absence pure and simple of the narrator. I will come back to this in Chapter 15.

[7]*Great Expectations*, chapter 18.

[8]Hortense Hulot in *La Cousine Bette*, chapter 66 [trans. Marion Ayton Crawford (Harmondsworth: Penguin, 1965), p. 244].

than to quoting spoken words. The affinity between the free indirect and innermost thoughts is perhaps relatively greater, but those two seem to me by no means inseparable, and Flaubert's work abounds in striking counterexamples. Much has also been made (by the Vosslerians again, and by Hernadi and Pascal) of the value of empathy—the famous ambiguity—between narrator and character; Bally and Bronzwaer rightly dispute this, however, pointing out the almost systematic presence of de-ambiguitizing markers and the often ironic usage (Flaubert, Mann) of this technique.[9] The absolutely undecidable statements are actually extremely rare,[10] and Banfield[11] makes clear that such ambiguities refer us less to an identity of thought between characters and narrator than to an impossible choice between two interpretations that are *nonetheless incompatible,* as in the famous trick drawings analyzed by Gombrich. From the fact that the text does not always say whether the character or the narrator is speaking, it does not necessarily follow that they are thinking the same thing.

The last point of controversy concerns mimetic capacity, or aptitude for literal (re)production. Here, too, the main point seems to me beyond all argument—namely, that in this respect the capacity of free indirect style is inferior to that of direct style and superior to that of the governed indirect: "not only grammatically intermediate . . . ," says McHale, "but

[9]That such ironies may not always be perceived by incompetent or hostile readers is an occupational hazard. Eugen Lerch supposes, a little hyperbolically but not unreasonably, that *Bovary* owed its trial for immorality to some of Emma's thoughts in the free indirect that were attributed tendentiously to Flaubert.

[10]An example (obviously made up): "I decided to marry Albertine: I was definitely in love with her." In contrast, an "I was in love with her *once and for all*" would be de-ambiguitized (assigned simply to the hero's naiveté) by the subsequent events of the novel.

[11]Ann Banfield, "The Formal Coherence of Represented Speech and Thought," *PTL* 3 (1978), 305.

also mimetically intermediate."[12] Hernadi, too, substitutes for the traditional opposition *diégésis/mimésis* a three-term gradation in which the free indirect, under the name of "substitutionary narration," occupies the middle. McHale proposes a more complex gradation, whose seven degrees of increasing "mimeticism" are laid out pretty much as follows (pp. 258–259): (1) the "diegetic summary," which mentions the verbal act without specifying its content, as in this example (which is my substitution, as are all the subsequent ones): "Marcel spoke to his mother for an hour"; (2) the "summary, less purely diegetic," specifying the content: "Marcel informed his mother of his decision to marry Albertine";[13] these first two degrees correspond to my "narratized speech"; (3) "indirect content-paraphrase" (governed indirect speech): "Marcel declared to his mother that he wanted to marry Albertine"; (4) (governed) "indirect discourse, mimetic to some degree," faithful to certain stylistic aspects of the discourse being (re)produced: "Marcel declared to his mother that he wanted to marry that little bitch, Albertine"; (5) "free indirect discourse": "Marcel went and confided to his mother: he absolutely had to marry Albertine"; these three degrees correspond to my "transposed speech"; (6) "direct discourse": "Marcel said to his mother, 'I must marry Albertine'"; (7) "free direct discourse," without any demarcating signs; this is the *autonomous* state of "immediate speech": "Marcel goes to see his mother. I must marry Albertine" (this form would not be very plausible in Proust but has been common currency ever since Joyce); the last two degrees correspond to my "reported speech."

This distribution seems to me extremely sensible, and I willingly concur with it except for the reservation that the

---

[12][McHale, "Free Indirect Discourse," p. 259.]

[13]A real example in Balzac: "And for ten minutes he poured out his fury" (*La Cousine Bette*, chapter 20 [Penguin, p. 86]).

term "free direct discourse" may indicate a factitious or specious symmetry between the various states of direct and indirect speech. This symmetry, already implied by other critics,[14] was put into words by Strauch, who distinguishes in each of those types a governed state and an ungoverned state. The distinction, obviously relevant to the indirect, is hardly so to the direct, which by definition is never *governed* but is only introduced by a declarative verb or signaled by quotation marks or a dash, or both introduced and signaled. The "free direct" is free only in that it dispenses with those marks without any resultant grammatical effect and therefore without real government. Understood in this way, the term "free direct" is obviously useful for designating the most emancipated and, in the modern novel, the most characteristic forms of dialogue and monologue. *Ulysses* is strewn with them.

Another reservation bears on the automatic and unavoidable nature of this gradation of mimetic effects. Its validity is somewhat that of a statistical norm, and depending on the context, it admits of many transgressions, exceptions, and inversions. The contract of literalness implied by the use of direct discourse is not always respected and can be broken by the narrative context; and inversely, the appearance of paraphrase can mask a literal quotation. Some illustrations of that paradox can be found in the recent article by Meir Sternberg,[15] which is a useful warning against any dogmatic or mechanistic attitude in this area.

[14]See McHale, "Free Indirect Discourse," p. 259.
[15]Meir Sternberg, "Proteus in Quotation-Land: Mimesis and the Forms of Reported Discourse," *Poetics Today* 3 (1982), 107–156.

10 *Narrative of Thoughts?*

Dorrit Cohn's third criticism[1] bears on the assimilation I made (at least from the viewpoint of narrative treatment) of thought to speech, viewing all "consciousness" as if it consisted of inner speech. This criticism is inseparable from her own work, whose aim is, precisely, to create for the "presentation of consciousness" the special place it deserves, and so I cannot respond to her criticism without saying something about her book itself.

Remember, first, that for Dorrit Cohn the three basic techniques of the presentation of consciousness are *psycho-narration*, the analysis of a character's thoughts taken on directly by the narrator; *quoted monologue*, a literal citation of those thoughts as they are verbalized in inner speech, of which the "interior monologue" is only a more autonomous variant; and finally, *narrated monologue*, monologue relayed by the narrator in the form of indirect discourse, governed or free. It is clear that except for our difference in scope (Cohn is not concerned with speeches actually uttered), her categories and mine are completely interchangeable, but the interchange reveals three differences.

The first bears on choice of terms: her "psycho-narration" is

---

[1]Cohn, *Transparent Minds*, p. 24 and passim.

my "narratized speech," her "quoted monologue" is my "reported speech," and her "narrated monologue" is my "transposed speech." I confess that I fail to perceive the advantage of this modification. "Narrated" seems to me too strong (and thus too close to -*narrative*) to refer to indirect discourse, and I persist in reserving it for the forms (of the kind "I decided to marry Albertine") that treat speech or thought as an event,[2] while retaining "transposed," whose grammatical connotation is clear, for indirect speech.

The second difference bears on the order she selected. Several times Dorrit Cohn calls her "narrated monologue" an *intermediate* mode, so I fail to understand why she places it third. I prefer to leave it in the second spot, to which I assigned it in what is indeed a systematic progression.

The third disagreement results from the radical separation Dorrit Cohn makes between "third-person" and "first-person" narratives and from the prime strategic importance she attributes to that separation. It governs the two parts of her book (I. "Consciousness in Third-Person Context"; II. "Consciousness in First-Person Texts"), and to a certain extent it leads her to deal with the same forms twice, depending on whether they occur in a hetero- or a homodiegetic narration. It seems to me, however, that formally the encompassing narrative situation has no effect on the status of either the discourse or the psychic state evoked. I scarcely see what

[2]In a letter to A. Bosquet (*Correspondance*, ed. Conard, V, 321), Flaubert advised "recounting" the *words* of a secondary character. This term gives a little backing to my "narratized," but to tell the truth we don't know whether here it applies to narratization strictly speaking (as when, in *Bovary*, "'You are not right,' said the hostess, 'he is an excellent man'" becomes "the hostess said some words in the curé's defense" [Modern Library Edition, trans. Francis Steegmuller, p. 88]) or to a plain indirect discourse, which is Flaubert's most frequent position—in short, whether he is using my terminology or Dorrit Cohn's. See Claudine Gothot-Mersch, *Travail de Flaubert* (Paris: Seuil, 1983).

(other than the grammatical person, of course) distinguishes, for example, *auto-*(psycho)*narration* from *psycho-narration*, auto-narrated monologue from (hetero)narrated monologue. I have particular difficulty understanding why Dorrit Cohn links her study of autonomous monologue to first-person narrative: *Ulysses* taken as a whole is not, to my knowledge, a first-person novel. If her reason is that Molly Bloom's monologue is *in itself* in the first person, the reason is meaningless, because Molly Bloom's monologue is no more in the first person than are the (non-autonomous) quoted monologues present in the classical heterodiegetic novel, which she correctly deals with in her first part. This peculiarity of distribution seems to me to be due to a misplaced desire to divide up—that is, to an overvaluation of the criterion of person.[3] We will come back to this far-reaching difference apropos of voice.

The fourth and final difference, which I mentioned earlier and to which I now return, is the assimilation—which I made and which Dorrit Cohn, rightly, rejects—of "consciousness" to inner speech. Cohn legitimately insists on making a place for the nonverbal forms of consciousness, and I was certainly wrong to classify as "narratized inner *speech*" a statement such as "I decided to marry Albertine," which is by no means necessarily tied to a verbalized thought. A fortiori, no doubt, for something like "I fell in love with Albertine." But I note that, of the three modes of presentation differentiated by Cohn, only the first makes a place for this question; by definition, quoted monologue and narrated monologue treat thought as speech, in her work as in mine (and once again, that is why "narrated" here seems to me ill chosen or, rather,

---

[3]Several times, moreover, Dorrit Cohn recognizes the identity of problems in the two types of narrative situation (pp. 14, 143, 158, 169); and the fundamental opposition between consonance and dissonance (of character and narrator) plays the same role in both parts of her book.

ill placed). Only "psycho-narration" may be assumed to apply to a nonverbal thought (falling in love with Albertine, or with anyone else, without *saying so to oneself* or, indeed, without being aware of it).[4] But note that I say: *may.* Falling in love with Albertine, or with her neighbor, *may also* consist of an inner speech, and on this point the psycho-narrative statement says neither yea nor nay, except perhaps when it takes pains to mark the unconscious nature of the state represented. If a narrator writes, "Marcel, *without noticing it,* had fallen in love with Albertine," he takes the exceptional step of letting us know that the sentence "So now I am in love with Albertine" does not appear in Marcel's inner speech—which still falls short of ensuring that such speech is absent. Marcel might, in such a case, "say to himself" other sentences, and particularly this one: "I am *not* in love with Albertine"— which the perspicacious narrator decodes for him.

In short, Dorrit Cohn's justifiable reservation about a possible nonverbalized consciousness holds good only *partly* for *one* of her three categories. Let us arbitrarily figure this part at 1/2: Cohn's reservation holds good for 1/6 of her own system. I will not be petty enough to deduce from this that I am 5/6 right in disagreeing with her. I will, rather, conclude that the narrative of thoughts (since that, indeed, is what we are dealing with) always and completely comes down either, as I was too quick to say, to a narrative of words or—as I ought to have said with respect to the cases in which it does not *with its own technique* set forth these thoughts as verbal— to a *narrative of events.* Once again, narrative recognizes only events or speeches (which are a particular type of event, the only type that may be directly *quoted* in a verbal narrative). In

[4]Obviously, this is not a matter of taking sides on the stale exam question "Is there thought without language?" but only of making a place for the forms of "representation" that do not decide that question in the negative.

verbal narrative, "consciousness" can be only one or the other.

To this blunt dichotomy, Doležel and Schmid add another, to which I have already alluded. In a narrative, they say, there are and there can be only two sorts of text: the text of the narrator (*Erzählertext*) or the text of a character (*Personentext*). It may be tempting to line up these two oppositions as equivalents; that is what Pierre van den Heuvel does. But things are not so simple. My dichotomy is *by object,* Doležel's is *by mode,* and the two are not reducible, for some narratives of events can be taken on by a character and some narratives of words can be taken on by the narrator. So it would be better to dissociate the criteria and to have them intersect in one of those double-entry tables with which I have not yet had the opportunity of embellishing this little book. In such a table we would differentiate between the narrative of events as taken on by the narrator's discourse (primary narrative with an extradiegetic narrator) and the narrative of events as taken on by a character's discourse (secondary narrative with an intradiegetic narrator, or a character-narrator) and between the narrative of words as taken on by the narrator's discourse (either narratized or transposed discourse) and the narrative of words as taken on by a character's discourse (either reported or transposed discourse). So we would have this grid:

Object \ Mode	Narrator's discourse	Character's discourse
Events	Primary narrative	Secondary narrative
Words	Narratized speech and transposed speech	Reported speech and transposed speech

As one can see, I put "transposed speech" (indirect styles) into two slots at once; I had hesitated and begun to envis-

age—a sorry choice—an intermediate slot. But taking everything into consideration, I think that with its "dual" voice, it
well deserves to be entered doubly.

Moreover, persisting in my erroneous ways, I did not grant
a third row to the narrative of thoughts. I have already said
why, but it is worth repeating: narrative always reduces
thoughts either to speeches or to events. It leaves no room for
a third term, and, once more, this lack of gradation—which is
narrative's doing and not mine—results from its own verbal
nature. Narrative, which tells stories, is concerned only with
events; certain of those events are verbal; in that case, as an
exception for the sake of variety, narrative happens to *reproduce* them. But it has no other choice, and consequently
neither do we.

11   *Perspective*

The distinction between the two questions "Who sees?" (a question of mood) and "Who speaks?" (a question of voice) is generally accepted today, at least in principle. My only regret is that I used a purely visual, and hence overly narrow, formulation. The end of the scene between Charlus and Jupien in *Sodome I* is indeed focalized through Marcel, but that focalization is auditory. There would have been no point in taking tion is auditory. There would have been no point in taking great pains to replace *point of view* with *focalization* if I was only going to fall right back into the same old rut; so obviously we must replace *who sees?* with the broader question of *who perceives?* But the very symmetry between "Who perceives?" and "Who speaks?" is perhaps slightly factitious: the narrator's voice is indeed always conveyed as the voice of a person, even if anonymous, but the focal position, when there is one, is not always identified with a person. That, it seems to me, is the case with external focalization. So perhaps it would be better to ask, in a more neutral way, *where is the focus of perception?*—and this focus may or may not (and I will return to this) be embodied in a character.

My criticism of earlier classifications (Brooks and Warren, Stanzel, Friedman, Booth, Romberg) obviously bears on the confusion they produced between mood and voice, either

(Friedman, Booth) by christening "narrator" a focal character who never opens his mouth[1] or by classifying complex narrative situations (mood + voice) under the heading of "point of view." That is obviously the case for Brooks and Warren, Friedman, and Booth, but indeed much less so for Stanzel and Romberg, whom we can reproach only for presenting differences in point of view and differences in narrative enunciating as if the two were equivalent.

But the common and sometimes glaring confusion between mood and voice, focalization and narration, is one thing; bringing mood and voice together within the more complex (synthetic) idea of "narrative situation" is something else. I acknowledged (pp. 188–189) this synthesis as legitimate, but I rightly refused to consider it "here"—that is, under the single heading of "point of view." I thereby implicitly committed myself to considering it elsewhere and did not honor that commitment in *Narrative Discourse*. A little later I will try to make good the omission.

My study of focalizations has caused much ink to flow—no doubt, a little too much. It was never anything but a reformulation, whose main advantage was to draw together and systematize such standard ideas as "narrative with an omniscient narrator" or "vision from behind" (zero focalization); "narrative with point of view, reflector, selective omniscience, restriction of field" or "vision with" (internal focalization); or "objective,[2] behaviorist technique" or "vision from

---

[1]As Dorrit Cohn rightly says, it is proper to "put a stop . . . to the sloppy habit of calling the protagonists of figural novels (Stephen of the *Portrait*, Gregor Samsa, or Strether) the 'narrators' of their stories" ("Encirclement of Narrative," p. 171).

[2]The importance of this typically modern mode was, I think, first pointed out in France by Claude-Edmonde Magny in *L'Age du roman américain* (Paris: Seuil, 1948) in the chapter "La Technique objective." Magny's study is slighted today; people often steal from it without acknowledging, and sometimes without being aware, that they are doing so. Yet in many respects it

without" (external focalization). My own contribution lay in the study of those "alterations" of the dominant modal course of a narrative to which we have given the names *paralipsis* (the holding back of information that would be logically produced under the type of focalization selected) and *paralepsis* (information in excess of what is called for by the logic of the type selected).

Once or twice people have noted in my pages some confusion between mood and voice—a "pre-Genettean" sin, as Mieke Bal says, that I ought to be the last person to commit (or rather, if history moves forward, the first person to stop committing). I sinned at least by ellipsis or imprecision.

First, in the examples I gave of multiple focalization (epistolary novel, *The Ring and the Book*), the change in focus is manifestly accompanied—and I ought at least to have said so—by a change in narrator, and there the transfocalization may seem simply a consequence of the transvocalization. Moreover, I know of no example of pure transfocalization, where "the same story" is told successively from several points of view but by the same heterodiegetic narrator. That would, however, be more interesting, for the presumed objectivity of the narrating would, as in movies, accentuate the effect of dissonance among versions. That challenge remains to be met, the sooner the better.

Next, apropos of external focalization in Hammett, I ought to have said explicitly that it functions sometimes (*The Glass Key*, *The Maltese Falcon*) in heterodiegetic narration, sometimes (*The Dain Curse*, *Red Harvest*, *The Thin Man*) in homodiegetic narration. I will come back to this, but for me it

---

was the starting point of French narratology, which was stimulated by its juxtaposition of the American novel and cinematographic technique. Its omission from the bibliography of *Narrative Discourse* is entirely typical—and all the more unjustifiable since, after reading and admiring the book when it was first published, I drew attention to it in 1966 in the dossier of *Communications* 8 (1966), 166. An intermittent memory.

does indeed prove the relative autonomy of choices of mood in relation to choices of voice, and reciprocally. The same comment apropos of the celebrated paralipsis in *Roger Ackroyd:* Shlomith Rimmon reproaches me for citing that novel as an example of focalization through the hero (the murderer) "without mentioning the fact that the focus-murderer is also the narrator, when this is clearly the main 'trick' used in the novel."[3] I do not share her way of looking at it. The trick here lies in the paralipsis—that is, in the omission of essential information that focalization through the murderer ought to include. The fact of entrusting the narrating to him is only a way of emphasizing and, if one wishes, of ensuring that focalization—and consequently that paralipsis.[4] And I persist in thinking that a clearly indicated heterodiegetic internal focalization, as in *The Ambassadors* or *Portrait of the Artist,* would have produced the same effect.

External focalization was certainly not invented by the writers of American novels between the two world wars. They broke new ground only by maintaining external focalization throughout the entire length of a narrative, generally a brief

---

[3]Shlomith Rimmon, "A Comprehensive Theory of Narrative: G. Genette's *Figures III* and the Structuralist Study of Fiction," *PTL* 1 (1976), 59.

[4]This is more or less Roland Barthes's opinion in his "Introduction à l'analyse structurale des récits": "The device," he says, after considering it in *The Sittaford Mystery,* also by Agatha Christie, where the paraliptic cheating functions in the third person, "is still more blatant in *The Murder of Roger Ackroyd,* since there the murderer actually says *I*" (in *Poétique du récit* [Paris: Seuil, 1977], pp. 41 and 56 [tr. "Introduction to the Structural Analysis of Narratives," in *Image—Music—Text,* trans. Stephen Heath (New York: Hill & Wang, 1977), p. 113]). In *Degree Zero,* Barthes's point of view was closer to Rimmon's: ". . . a novel by Agatha Christie in which all the invention consisted in concealing the murderer beneath the use of the first person of the narrative. The reader looked for him behind every 'he' in the plot: he was all the time hidden under the 'I.' Agatha Christie knew perfectly well that, in the novel, the 'I' is usually a spectator, and that it is the 'he' who is the actor" (*Le Degré zéro de l'écriture* [Paris: Seuil, 1953; rpt. 1972], p. 28 [tr. *Writing Degree Zero,* trans. Annette Lavers and Colin Smith (1964; rpt. Boston: Beacon Press, 1970), pp. 34–35]).

one. I drew attention (pp. 190–191) to the classical novel's use of external focalization in introductions, and I contrasted that practice, "still" manifest in *Germinal*, with the practice James followed in his late novels, where the character whose presence opens the action is presumed at the very start to be known. I was suggesting a historical evolution about which I had scarcely more than a wholly intuitive view; I was also naively setting foot in a sensitive area that had already been investigated. Let me add just a word or two on the subject.

The historical study I called for is currently being undertaken only, to my knowledge, by Jaap Lintvelt at Groningen; his investigation bears on the beginnings of modern novels. I had in mind particularly a verification (or refutation) of my historical hypothesis of a change having occurred in the second half of the nineteenth century; and with the help of a three-year-old child, I undertook a spot check of some major novels from the seventeenth century to the twentieth. If we roughly contrast two types of *incipit*—type A (which assumes the character to be unknown to the reader, looks at him first from the outside—thus taking on, in a way, the reader's ignorance—and then formally introduces him, as in *Peau de chagrin*) and type B (which at the outset assumes the character to be known and immediately refers to him by his name, even his first name, even simply a personal pronoun or a "familiarizing"[5] definite article)—we note that the history of the

---

[5]Bronzwaer, referred to by Stanzel ("Teller-Characters and Reflector-Characters in Narrative Theory," *Poetics Today* 2 [1981], 11). (In a term that is very metonymical but very eloquent, Damourette and Pichon, I think, call the definite article "notorious" [Jacques Damourette and Edouard Pichon, *Des mots à la pensée: Essai de grammaire de la langue française*, 7 vols., Paris, Collection des linguistes contemporains, 1911–1940].) On the focalizing value of characters' names, see Boris Uspenski (*A Poetics of Composition* [Berkeley: University of California Press, 1973]). There is, indeed, no question but that calling his heroine *Madame Bovary*, or *Madame*, or *Emma* can express the narrator's degrees of familiarity and/or the choice of one or another focal character.

modern novel shows a significant evolution. Roughly speaking, it consists of a transition from type A, which predominates[6] up to but not including Zola (but it is still present, then, in *La Fortune des Rougon, Nana, Pot-Bouille,* and *Germinal*), to type B, which is already represented in *La Curée* (of the twenty *Rougon-Macquart* novels, fourteen are distinct cases of type B). In James we find a clear transition, from a predominance of A up to *The Bostonians* to a predominance of B dating from *Casamassima* (both published in 1885) and on to the end. The turning point, perhaps provisionally, is indeed, therefore, located in that zone, let us say symbolically 1885. The use of type B is striking in the twentieth century in such novels as *Ulysses, The Trial* or *The Castle, Les Thibault, La Condition humaine,* or *Aurélien,* and the novella is apt to take the elliptical introduction so far as to use a simple pronoun or definite article ("Hills Like White Elephants": "*The* American and *the* girl . . ."). That practice is rarer, perhaps, in the novel, but it is used in *For Whom the Bell Tolls* ("*He* lay flat . . ."),[7] and in 1900 Conrad opened *Lord Jim* with a "He" that only after a full page becomes a very discreet "Jim": "Jim had always good wages . . . just Jim—nothing more. He had, of course, another name, but he was anxious that it should not

[6]In the extreme form of an external focalization in which the ignorance is conspicuous and is emphasized by an observer's assumptions ("by his appearance one recognized," "by his physiognomy one guessed," etc.), as in *La Peau de chagrin, Pons, Bette, Le Médecin de campagne, Splendeurs et misères;* or in the form (also frequent in Balzac) of a descriptive and/or historical panoramic opening: *Goriot, Grandet, Illusions perdues, Curé de village, Recherche de l'absolu, Vieille Fille,* etc.

[7]On the familiarizing effect *for the reader* of that narrative stance, see Walter Ong, "The Writer's Audience Is Always a Fiction," *PMLA* 90 (1975), 12–15. As Father Ong shows full well, these allusive designations (pseudo-anaphorics or pseudo-deictics) force the reader into a relationship of intimacy and complicity with the author—a relationship the reader is prevented from refusing (by even so much as an "uncooperative" question like "Who is this 'he'? What American? What girl?") by the sly intimidation that is inherent (as we would say today) in all presupposition.

be pronounced"—and, if I am not mistaken, in actual fact it never will be, for us.

These openings that use pronouns have been studied by J. M. Backus, who speaks of "nonsequential sequence-signals":[8] referentials without reference, anaphorics without antecedents, but whose function is precisely to simulate, and thereby to *constitute*, a reference, and to impose it on the reader by way of presupposition. Roland Harweg, using Pike's terms, contrasts "emic" openings (with a character's name) and "etic" openings (with only a pronoun).[9] But the question transcends the use of pronouns or definite articles. A simple pronoun is obviously more "etic" than a complete denomination (first and last names), which itself is more "etic" than a formal introduction coming after the "tracking shot" of the Balzacian novel. There is in fact a whole gradation, with subtle and variable nuances depending on context, from the pole of most explicitness (à la Balzac: "June 15, 1952, at five o'clock, a young woman emerged from an elegant hotel located at 54 rue de Varenne, . . ." and, after a few pages of description, "This elegant woman walking was none other than the Marquise of . . .") to the pole of most implicitness (à la Duras: "She saw that it was five o'clock. She went out . . ."), with Valéry's formulation definitely an intermediary degree: "The Marquise."[10] What Marquise? As Stanzel remarks, the etic or implicit pole is obviously closely related

---

[8]J. M. Backus, "'He Came into Her Line of Vision Walking Backward': Nonsequential Sequence-Signals in Short Story Openings," *Language Learning* 15 (1965), 67–83.

[9]Roland Harweg, *Pronomina und Textkonstitution* (Munich: Fink, 1968), pp. 152–166 and 317–323.

[10][Oral tradition attributes to Valéry the quip, "I could never write a novel, for I could never write a sentence like 'The Marquise went out at five o'clock.'"]

to his own "figural" narrative type—that is, to internal focalization—and therefore to a certain novelistic modernity.[11]

The investigation, of course, remains open and ought to take into account both individual and generic details. The novella, as we have seen and for obvious reasons, is more elliptical than the novel; the historical novel can be more elliptical than pure fiction, since some of its characters are by definition assumed to be "well known." Formal details ought also to be taken into account, and here homodiegetic narrating introduces a special feature: the pronoun *I* is both etic and emic, since we know at least that it designates the narrator. But it certainly seems to have undergone the same general evolution, from the formal presentation of the picaresque novel ("Your Excellency, then, should know first of all that I am called Lázaro de Tormes, son of Thomé González"[12]) to Proustian ellipsis, by way of Melville's casual familiarity ("Call me Ishmael").

[11]Stanzel, "Teller-Characters and Reflector-Characters," p. 11.

[12][*The Life of Lazarillo de Tormes*, trans. Harriet de Onís (Woodbury, N.Y.: Barron's Educational Series, 1959).]

12 Focalizations

My definition of the types of focalization was criticized and overhauled by Mieke Bal on the basis of what seems to me an unreasonable desire to set up focalization as a narrative *instance* (or agent). Mieke Bal seems to have—and sometimes to attribute to me (p. 248)[1]—the idea that every narrative statement includes a *focalizer* (character) and a *focalized* (character). In her view, in internal focalization the focalized character is at the same time the focalizer ("the 'focalized' character sees"), but in external focalization, the focalized character is only focalized ("he does not see, he is seen"). And (still according to her) I conceal this asymmetry by my "nonchalant" use of the expression "focalization on" [focalisation sur][2] instead of "focalization by," which allegedly leads me to "treat . . . Phileas and his valet as almost interchangeable agents—treating the subject (Passepartout) or the object (Phileas) alike as 'focalized'" (p. 241). I find it quite difficult to enter into this argument, for in her statement of my position, Mieke Bal in-

---

[1]For example, *Narratologie*, p. 37. The gist of the discussion is in the first chapter, to which I refer in the following pages. [Page numbers in the text are to "The Narrating and the Focalizing."]

[2][In *Narrative Discourse*, "focalisation sur" was rendered as "focalization through."]

troduces ideas (*focalizer, focalized*) I never thought of using because they are incompatible with my conception of the matter. For me, there is no focalizing or focalized character: *focalized* can be applied only to the narrative itself, and if *focalizer* applied to anyone, it could only be the person who *focalizes the narrative*—that is, the narrator, or, if one wanted to go outside the conventions of fiction, the *author* himself, who delegates (or does not delegate) to the narrator his power of focalizing or not focalizing.

In her debate with Bronzwaer, Mieke Bal denies I admit the existence of "nonfocalized passages" and claims I specify that such a category is applicable only to narratives taken as a whole.[3] That obviously means that the analysis of a "nonfocalized" narrative must always be reducible to a mosaic of variously focalized segments and, therefore, that "*zero focalization*" = *variable focalization*. That formula would not bother me in the least, but it seems to me that classical narrative sometimes places its "focus" at a point so indefinite, or so remote, with so panoramic a field (the well-known "viewpoint of God," or of Sirius, about which people periodically wonder whether it is indeed a point of view) that it cannot coincide with any character and that the term nonfocalization, or zero focalization, is rather more appropriate for it. Unlike the director of a movie, the novelist is not compelled to put his camera somewhere; he has no camera.[4] Instead,

---

[3]Mieke Bal, "The Laughing Mice, or: On Focalization," *Poetics Today* 2 (1981), 205. [Bal's statement was that "Genette (recognizes unfocalized passages) but in relation to a definition of focalization as a typology of texts, not as an indispensable narrative device."]

[4]It is true that today he may pretend to have one (the return effect of one medium on another). On the difference between focalization and "ocularization" (information and perception) and on the usefulness of this distinction for the technique of movies and the Nouveau Roman, see François Jost, "Narration(s): en deçà et au-delà," *Communications* 38 (1983), and "Du nouveau roman au nouveau romancier: Questions de narratologie," thesis

therefore, the right formula would be: *zero focalization = variable, and sometimes zero, focalization*. Here as elsewhere, the choice is purely operational. This looseness will undoubtedly shock some people, but I see no reason for requiring narratology to become a catechism with a yes-or-no answer to check off for each question, when often the proper answer would be that it depends on the day, the context, and the way the wind is blowing.

So by focalization I certainly mean a restriction of "field"— actually, that is, a selection of narrative information with respect to what was traditionally called *omniscience*. In pure fiction that term is, literally, absurd (the author has nothing to "know," since he invents everything), and we would be better off replacing it with *completeness of information*—which, when supplied to a reader, makes him "omniscient." The instrument of this possible selection is a *situated focus*, a sort of information-conveying pipe that allows passage only of information that is authorized by the situation (Marcel on his steep slope outside the window at Montjouvain). In internal focalization, the focus coincides with a character, who then becomes the fictive "subject" of all the perceptions, including those that concern himself as object. The narrative in that case *can* tell us everything this character perceives and everything he thinks (it never does, either because it refuses to give irrelevant information or because it deliberately withholds some bit of relevant information [paralipsis], like the moment and the memory of the crime in *Roger Ackroyd*). In principle it is *supposed* to tell us nothing else. If it does, that is again an alteration (paralepsis), in other words, an infraction, inten-

---

(Ecole des Hautes Etudes en Sciences Sociales, Paris, 1983), chapter 3 ("La Mobilité narrative"). Turning back from those extreme cases to the ordinary condition of narrative, I find Jost's work the most relevant contribution to the debate on focalization and to the necessary refining of that notion.

tional or not, of the modal position of the moment, as when Marcel "perceives"—not *guesses*—Mlle Vinteuil's thoughts at Montjouvain. In external focalization, the focus is situated at a point in the diegetic universe chosen by the narrator, *outside every character*, which means that all possibility of information about anyone's thoughts is excluded—whence its advantage for certain modern novelists with a "behaviorist" bias. In principle, therefore, the two types of focalization cannot be confused, unless the author has constructed (focalized) his narrative in a manner that is not only incoherent but chaotic.

However, *from the point of view of the relevant information*, the two positions may on occasion be equivalent. That is what we have in the litigious example of the opening chapters of *Le Tour du monde en 80 jours*. I never treated Phileas and Passepartout "as almost interchangeable agents," as Mieke Bal has accused me of doing (moreover, I see no reason suddenly to name them "agents," but this is another question, to be considered in due course); and I never said Jules Verne's position could be called, at will, external focalization on Phileas or internal focalization through Passepartout (or any other particular witness). I suppose that these two positions alternate and that, for lack of enough detail, certain segments may remain indeterminable, but I will not take the trouble to go look, because that is not the point. The point is that, *so far as our information about Phileas is concerned*, the two positions are *equivalent* and that *in this respect* the distinction between them can be *disregarded*.

I find myself answering Mieke Bal here with the italics suitable for van Rees, and I can easily guess that such a comparison will not please her, but so it goes. They both reproach me for "nonchalance," and in both cases my defense is the same: without "nonchalance" toward details that are not relevant to the question at hand, plainly no research is possible, for research is nothing but a series of questions, and the point is not to ask the wrong question. In the case of *Le Tour du monde,* the point is that Phileas, *at that time the object of the narrative,*[5] is seen from the outside; whether the point of view lies with Passepartout, with an anonymous observer, or in the air somewhere is, at that moment, of only secondary importance; that is, its importance is, *for the moment, negligible.*

The rest of the Balian theory of focalizations develops according to its own logic, based on her innovation (establishment of an *instance of focalization* composed of a focalizer, a focalized, and even, page 251, "recipients of the focalizing"), whose usefulness escapes me and whose effects perplex me, like the idea of a *focalization in the second degree.* Thus, these two sentences from *La Chatte*—"She watched him drink and felt a sudden pang of desire at the sight of his mouth pressing against the rim of the glass. But he felt so weary that he refused to share that pang"[6]—contain, for Mieke Bal, an embedding of focalizations, with Alain being "focalized in the second degree, by the focalizer who is focalized [Camille]" (p. 252). For me, there is simply a change of focus or, better, a displacement of the focus (which is situated on Camille in the first sentence, on Alain in the second) plus an element that is elided but indispensable to the coherence of the passage— namely, the fact that Alain *perceives* Camille's pang of desire, which implies that he sees her looking at him: an embedding of looks, if one wishes, in a sense already very metaphorical (obviously!), but not of focalizations. I do see that a narrative may mention a glance that perceives another glance, and so on, but I do not believe the *focus* of the narrative can be at two

[5]The term *hero,* which I used on page 192, was obviously clumsy, and Mieke Bal is right to call attention to it. The object of a narrative is not necessarily always the "main character"—for example, Charles at the beginning of *Bovary.*

[6]["The Cat," trans. Antonia White, in *7 by Colette* (New York: Farrar, Straus & Cudahy, 1955), p. 72.]

points *simultaneously*. Certainly I am unable to demonstrate this. But it is up to Mieke Bal to demonstrate the contrary, and I am not aware that she has done so.[7]

A final comment on the matter of focalizations: at least twice (pp. 205 and 218) I used an expression that is fairly heterodox with respect to my own definitions, that of "focalization through the narrator," which I assert is "logically implied by the 'first-person' narrative." What we are obviously dealing with is the restricting of narrative information to the "knowledge" of the narrator *as such*—that is, to the information the hero has at that moment in the story as *completed by his subsequent information*, the whole remaining at the disposal of the hero-become-narrator. Only the hero at that moment in the story deserves *stricto sensu* the term "focalization"; for the hero-become-narrator, we are dealing with extradiegetic information, which only the identity of person between hero and narrator justifies us, *by extension*, in calling "focalization."

But here we have, indeed, one of those correlations between mood and voice that I have been rightly reproached for disregarding (for one must not disregard *everything*). Homodiegetic narration, by nature or convention (in this case, they amount to the same thing), simulates autobiography much more closely than heterodiegetic narration ordinarily simulates historical narrative. In fiction, the heterodiegetic narrator is not accountable for his information, "omniscience" forms part of his contract, and his motto might be this retort by a character of Prévert's: "What I don't know, I guess, and

[7]On this point and some others, the shortcomings of Mieke Bal's method seem to me successfully corrected in the article by Pierre Vitoux ("Le Jeu de la focalisation," *Poétique* 51 [1982], 359–368). But one inevitably thinks of the Ptolemaic system, which ended up unable to function without repairs that were so costly it was more expedient simply to do without the system. The question now, of course, is to know who is Ptolemy—and everyone believes himself to be Copernicus.

what I don't guess, I make up."[8] As for the homodiegetic narrator, he is obliged to justify ("How do you know that?") the information he gives about scenes from which "he" was absent as a character, about someone else's thoughts, etc., and any breach of that trust is a paralepsis. This is manifestly the situation for Bergotte's deathbed thoughts, which absolutely no one but Bergotte could know, and it is less distinctly the situation for many other people's thoughts, which there is little likelihood of Marcel's ever having come to know. We could therefore say that homodiegetic narrative, as a consequence of its "vocal" selection, submits a priori to a modal restriction, one that can be sidestepped only by an infraction, or a perceptible distortion. To designate that constraint, perhaps we should speak of *prefocalization?* Well, now we have.

[8]Meir Sternberg (*Expositional Modes,* chapters 8 and 9) opportunely distinguishes, among these omniscient narrators, the *omnicommunicative* narrators (who apparently give the reader all the information they have—see Trollope's novels) and the *suppressive* narrators (who hold back part, whether explicitly or not, permanently or not, etc., by ellipses or paralipses—see *Tom Jones*). But of course this distinction is equally well applicable to focalized narratives (see *Roger Ackroyd*).

13 *Voice*

The chapter on voice is unquestionably the one that (for me) provoked the most crucial discussions, at least apropos of the category of *person*. I have no intention of retracting my generalizations about the narrating instance or my thoughts about the time of the narrating, except—apropos of "subsequent" narrating—to moderate the view that the use of the preterite "inevitably" marks the story as prior.[1] The obviousness of that, as I myself mentioned, had been heatedly disputed a quarter of a century ago by Käte Hamburger, preceded, moreover, by Roland Barthes, who pointed out in *Degree Zero* that the preterite serves more to connote the literariness of the narrative than to denote the past of the action. For Käte Hamburger, as we know, the "epic preterite" has no temporal value: it marks only the fictiveness of fiction. This argument is undoubtedly not meant to be taken literally, and even less is it meant to be applied to every type of narrative in the past tense. To begin with, Hamburger herself by no means expects it to be applied to homodiegetic narrative, which she unhesitatingly places outside the sphere of fiction. It is self-evident, indeed, that a first-person narrative, at least

---

[1]On p. 219, and as early as p. 28.

when it takes the extended form of autobiography, explicitly locates its story in a completed past that fully marks its narrating as subsequent.[2]

I would readily say as much for certain heterodiegetic narratives that, with an epilogue in the present tense, are no less explicit in indicating the completed nature of their action. The epilogue unavoidably moves everything that has preceded back into the past—see *Tom Jones, Eugénie Grandet,* or *Madame Bovary.* For the latter, one may allege its partially homodiegetic nature, which is indicated, as we know, in the first chapter and is implicitly restored in the narrative's final sentences, which are in the present. To tell the truth, I think every ending in the present (and every beginning in the present, if it is not purely descriptive and sets the scene, as in *Père Goriot* or *Le Rouge et le noir*) introduces a measure of—let's say it—*homodiegeticity* into the narrative, since it positions the narrator as a contemporary and therefore, more or less, as a witness. That, quite obviously, is one of the transitions between the two types of narrative situation. From that angle, therefore, the two points of resistance to Käte Hamburger's argument may be reduced to just one.

A third alleged exception concerns the so-called historical narrative (of fiction). The term is certainly very indefinite, or at least here I think it has to be taken in the broadest possible sense, as covering every type of narrative (a) that is explicitly placed (even by only one date) in a historical past, even a very recent one, and (b) whose narrator, on the basis of that single piece of information, sets himself up more or less as a historian and therefore (if I may attempt this very slight oxymoron) as a *subsequent witness.* There is no need to say that

[2]This is less obvious for certain short homodiegetic narratives, like Hemingway's "Fifty Grand" or the novellas of Hammett, in which the narrative system gives very little sign of the presence of an "I" who is exceptionally discreet (I will come back to this) and therefore impersonal.

virtually all classical novels, from *La Princesse de Clèves* to *Les Géorgiques*, are included in this group,[3] or that this third exception has much in common with the other two. A subsequent witness is still a witness, and the "historical novelist," however distant the diegesis is from his narrative, is never entirely without some spatio-temporal relationship (however remote) to that diegesis.

Hamburger's argument, after all, is intended to hold true only for pure fiction, and fiction is rarely pure—more rarely, no doubt, than her thesis assumes; all the types I have just evoked are cases of impurity. In terms of our point of view here (which obviously has nothing to do with the more or less realistic nature of a narrative, for a novel may be simultaneously fantastic and situated in "real" history: see *Vathek* or *The Saragossa Manuscript*), pure fiction is a narrative devoid of all reference to a historical framework. Few novels, as I have said, fit that description, and perhaps no epic narrative does; and the "once upon a time" of folk tales seems to me to provide an unmistakable sign of the anteriority of the story, even though the story in question may be explicitly mythical. No doubt the novella most often illustrates the state of atemporality required for pure fiction; and we see how some of Hemingway's preterites approach the ideal state of an aorist without distance and without age.

Jaap Lintvelt, apropos of something else, draws attention to another infallible indication of subsequent narrating.[4] This is the presence (characteristic of what he calls the "authorial" narrative type) of "sure anticipations" in Lämmert's sense (*Zukunftgewissen Vorausdeutungen*): a narrator who, like *Eugénie Grandet*'s, announces, "In three days a terrible drama

[3] "All my novels," said Aragon, "are *historical* even though they are not in *costume*" (preface to *La Semaine sainte*).

[4] Jaap Lintvelt, *Essai de typologie narrative: Le Point de vue* (Paris: Corti, 1981), p. 54.

would begin . . ."[5] and who thereby, without any possibility of ambiguity, establishes his narrating act as posterior to the story he tells, or at least to the point in that story that he anticipates in this manner.

The use of the present tense might seem, a priori, most likely to simulate atemporality. (That is more or less its function, at least in French, in a widespread type of narrative that generally professes to be external to any historical reality: the "funny story" or joke.) But, in fact, the category of person plays a decisive role in the matter. In a heterodiegetic account (*Les Gommes*), the present may indeed have that atemporal value, but in a homodiegetic account (*Notes from the Underground*, Beckett's novels, *Dans le labyrinthe*), the value of simultaneity comes to the fore: the narrative recedes before the discourse and at every moment seems to be tipping over into "interior monologue." I mentioned this (*Narrative Discourse*, p. 219), but for a more detailed and discerning study of the effect, I can only refer to the chapter "From Narration to Monologue" in *Transparent Minds*.

But undoubtedly there is even more to it: if a beginning (*Père Goriot*) or an ending (*Eugénie Grandet*) in the present suffices to introduce a touch of homodiegeticity into a solidly heterodiegetic narrative, it would be a little paradoxical for us to deny this effect to a heterodiegetic narrating conducted[6] entirely in the present, as in *Les Gommes* or *Le Vice-Consul*. "Paradoxical," however, does not necessarily mean *erroneous*, for the claim may be made that in a wholly simultaneous narrating, the deictic value of the present (the *now* that suggests an *I*) is blunted and neutralized for lack of the contrast that, inversely, gives it so much force against a background in the past. Nevertheless, it seems to me that the effect of

[5][Penguin, p. 185.]

[6]I say *conducted* and not (entirely) *written* because here the basic present tense does not exclude analepses in the perfect or prolepses in the future.

homodiegeticization (if I may be so bold as to call it that) is never totally removed from a narrative in the present, whose tense always conveys more or less the presence of a narrator who—the reader unavoidably believes—cannot be very far from an action he himself presents as so near. That is obviously one of the elements of the *Jalousie*-effect. In short, I undoubtedly exaggerated a little the narrative consequences of using the past (a tense that does not always give the reader a very heightened feeling of the subsequentness of the narrating) and underestimated the narrative consequences of using the present (which almost irresistibly suggests the presence of a narrator in the diegesis).

14 *Level*

Just as the theory of focalizations was only a general presentation of the standard idea of "point of view," so the theory of narrative levels simply systematized the traditional notion of "embedding," whose main drawback is that it does not sufficiently mark the *threshold* between one diegesis and another—a threshold symbolized by the fact that the second diegesis is taken charge of by a narrative fashioned within the first diegesis. The weakness of that section of *Narrative Discourse*, or at least the obstacle to its comprehension, no doubt lies in the confusion that often develops between the attribute *extradiegetic*, which is a phenomenon of level, and the attribute *heterodiegetic*, which is a phenomenon of relation (of "person"). Gil Blas is an extradiegetic narrator because, albeit fictitious, he is included (*as narrator*) in no diegesis but is on an exactly equal footing with the extradiegetic (real) public; but since he tells his own story, he is at the same time a homodiegetic narrator. Inversely, Scheherazade is an intradiegetic narrator because before uttering a single word she is already a character in a narrative that is not her own; but since the story she tells is not about herself, she is at the same time a heterodiegetic narrator. "Homer" or "Balzac" are extra- and heterodiegetic; Ulysses or Des Grieux are intra- and homodiegetic. The crux of the confusion is undoubtedly an inadequate understanding of the prefix *extra*diegetic, which it seems paradoxical to attribute to a narrator who, like Gil Blas, is indeed present (as a character) in the story he recounts (as narrator, of course). But what matters here is that *as narrator* he is "off-diegesis," is situated outside of the diegesis, and that is all the prefix means. The most telling way to represent these relations of level would perhaps be to show the narrative embeddings by means of stick figures whose words, as in comic strips, are placed within balloon-shapes. Extradiegetic narrator (not character, for that would be meaningless) A (for example, the first narrator of *The Thousand and One Nights*) would produce a balloon—a first narrative with its diegesis— in which would appear an (intra)diegetic character B (Scheherazade); she, in turn, could become the narrator (still intradiegetic) of a metadiegetic narrative about a metadiegetic character C (Sinbad), who could possibly, in turn, etc.:

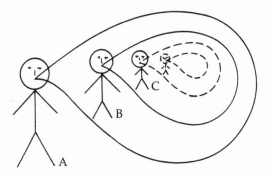

Once again, the relations of person freely cut across the relations of level, with no effect on their functioning. In *Manon Lescaut*, for example, the intradiegetic narrator and the metadiegetic character are the same person, Des Grieux, who for that reason is called the homodiegetic narrator. In the diagram we can symbolize that situation by doubling the letter-sign B, using the letter A to designate the extradiegetic narrator Renoncour:

Level

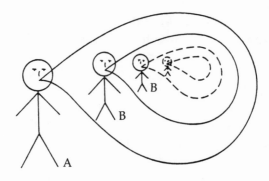

The section on *level* has, as far as I know, given rise to three criticisms. The first bore on substance but I mention it only as a reminder, for its author withdrew it almost immediately. In her excellent review of "Discours du récit," Shlomith Rimmon was of the opinion that in certain cases, determining the primary level (the extradiegetic narrating) could become problematic and that the system I proposed provided no criterion for making that determination:

> What, for example, is the primary narrative of Nabokov's *The Real Life of Sebastian Knight*? Is it Sebastian's reconstructed life or the narrator's quest for his half brother's biography? Any decision presupposes an interpretation, and objective criteria are not forthcoming. Moreover, sometimes the very structure of the work makes it impossible to decide which fictional level is primary and which secondary, an impossibility conducive to the creation of narrative ambiguity.
>
> What is missing in Genette's analysis is a set of properties which would help us detect the primary narrative and which in a case of narrative ambiguity would be equally applicable to two different levels.[1]

Some months later, studying head-on the questions of narra-

[1]Rimmon, "Comprehensive Theory of Narrative," pp. 59–60.

tive voice in *Sebastian Knight*, she reached the conclusion that the criteria of "Discours du récit" were sufficient for her analysis.[2] In fact (or rather, in truth), it seems to me that that novel presents no difficulty with respect to determining the primary level, which is obviously constituted by V's narrative. There would be a difficulty only if (and this confusion is standard) one were to interpret "primary narrative" ("primaire" or "premier") as meaning "thematically more important." But that issue, which in reality has to do with "interpretation," does not lie within the province of narratology. (In this respect, and stepping outside my present role, I will say—carefully between parentheses—that Sebastian seems to me in any case the character who is *most highly valued*, the one whom Nabokov invests with most of his arrogance. But a good enough share of it is left over for his biographer.)

I certainly do not claim that Shlomith Rimmon's retraction on this point puts the method of *Narrative Discourse* beyond all difficulty. There are probably narrative situations more complex or more perverse than *Sebastian Knight*'s—for example, the narrative situation of John Barth's "Menelaiad,"[3] which involves no fewer than seven narrative levels. But that work seems to me to create no more difficulty than Nabokov's: at the first level, an extradiegetic narrator—as he ought and without any possible ambiguity—addresses a narratee who is likewise extradiegetic.

The "narrative ambiguity" that Shlomith Rimmon envisaged is perhaps not so easy to produce, undoubtedly because the structures of language and the conventions of writing leave barely any room for it. One narrative can scarcely "embed" another without indicating the operation and, there-

[2]"Problems of Voice in V. Nabokov's *The Real Life of Sebastian Knight*," *PTL* 1 (1976), 489.

[3]In *Lost in the Funhouse* (New York: Doubleday, 1968); see *Palimpsestes*, pp. 391–392.

fore, without designating itself as the first narrative. *Can* the indicating and the designating be done silently or fallaciously? I confess my inability to conceive of this situation or to find actual examples of it, but that perhaps reveals only my ignorance, my lack of imagination, or the mental laziness of novelists, or even all three put together. What perhaps comes closest to such a situation in existing narratives is still that deliberate transgression of the threshold of embedding that we call *metalepsis*: when an author (or his reader) introduces himself into the fictive action of the narrative or when a character in that fiction intrudes into the extradiegetic existence of the author or reader, such intrusions disturb, to say the least, the distinction between levels. But the disturbance is so strong that it far transcends simple technical "ambiguity." It can be set down only to humor (Sterne, Diderot) or to the fantastic (Cortazar, Bioy Casares) or to some mixture of the two (Borges, of course[4]), unless it functions as a figure of the creative imagination—which it obviously does in the opening pages of *Noé*, where Giono shows the characters and décor of *Un Roi sans divertissement* crowding his attic desk while he wrote that novel.

Shlomith Rimmon envisages yet another difficulty, unless it be another formulation of the first one—that of novels "where there is only an intradiegetic narrator: what," she asks, "will the [extra]diegetic[5] level be in such cases?" At first

[4]Or Woody Allen: thanks to the help of a magician, Professor Kugelmass finds his way into the diegesis of *Madame Bovary* and becomes the lover of Emma, whom he brings back to twentieth-century New York. Finally, tired of her (like Rodolphe and Léon), he ships her back to Yonville. A little later, his magician inserts him by mistake into a new and not very novelistic diegesis(?): that of a Spanish grammar book, where he is awaited by very irregular verbs. During the metaleptic idyll, "'I cannot get my mind around this,' a Stanford professor said. 'First a strange character named Kugelmass, and now she's gone from the book. Well, I guess the mark of a classic is that you can reread it a thousand times and always find something new'" ("The Kugelmass Episode," in *Side Effects* [New York: Random House, 1975], p. 50).

[5]She said "diegetic" (p. 489) but no doubt that was a slip, since "diegetic" is synonymous with "*intra*diegetic."

glance, and for lack of examples, I have trouble seeing what she may have in mind and understanding the meaning of her question. A narrator can be perceived as intradiegetic only if he is presented as such by a narrative in which he appears, which constitutes precisely the level she claims to be seeking. But it is true that that frame narrative, at least in modern literature, can very well be resolved into a complete ellipsis. An example is *La Chute,* where Clamence's monologue in the presence of his silent listener can be "embedded" only implicitly in a frame narrative that is understood—that is clearly implied by all the statements in the monologue that relate not to the story it tells but to the circumstances of the narrating. Without its recourse to this implicit embedding, *La Chute* would escape the narrative mode,[6] since it consists wholly of one character's monologue or, more exactly (since that character is not alone but addresses a silent listener), of a long "tirade" without a rejoinder—a text in the dramatic mode, therefore, which one could, if no one has yet done it, bring to the stage without changing a word. The same effect can be produced—and in a more jolting and unexpected way—by taking a narrative that had seemed to have an extradiegetic narrator (and narratee) and tacking onto it a simple retort revealing *in extremis* that all along what we were dealing with was an intradiegetic narrative addressed to an actual listener: see the last line of *Portnoy.*[7]

The second criticism also comes from Shlomith Rimmon, who added, in her review:

[6]The narrative *mode* rather than the novelistic *genre:* the two boundaries do not merge with each other, and the novel—a "mixed" genre, as Plato said of the epic—can take on a purely dramatic form. All it has to do is consist exclusively of scenes in dialogue framed by no formula of presentation. So far as I am aware, that was the case with certain fashionable novels by Gyp at the beginning of this century and no doubt with some others.

[7]"So [*said the doctor*]. Now vee may perhaps to begin. Yes?" (Philip Roth, *Portnoy's Complaint* [New York: Random House, 1967], p. 274; brackets in the original). Certainly, throughout the text there is no lack of signs indicating the speaker's awareness of this singular narratee, the psychoanalyst

The term "primary narrative" ("*récit premier*") is perhaps also slightly misleading, since it may give the impression of defining the most important level, whereas in fact the metadiegetic level is often more important than the primary [primaire] narrative which can become little more than an excuse (e.g., *The Canterbury Tales*). It would perhaps be better to avoid talking of "primary" [premier] and "secondary" [second] narratives and to discuss the fictional levels in terms of depth of subordination.[8]

Rimmon is, of course, right to recall (as I, in turn, have just done) that the "embedded" narrative may be thematically more important than the one framing it (as is, indeed, most often the case), and here we come upon a difficulty we encountered before. At that time, apropos of questions of order, I proposed renaming my earlier "récit premier" as *récit primaire*. Apparently this is not enough of a precaution, since here Shlomith Rimmon is criticizing "premier" in its English form "primary," which would no doubt also serve as the translation of "primaire," but I hardly see any solution to this terminological problem—any more than the grammarians have found one for the fact that a "subordinate" clause may be thematically more important than the "main" clause. It is a fact that the embedded narrative is narratively subordinate to the embedding narrative, since the former owes its existence to the latter and is based on it. The opposition *primaire/second(aire)* conveys this fact in its own way, and we must, it seems to me, accept this contradiction between unquestionable narrative subordination and possible thematic precedence.

Spielvogel; but those signs are not enough to indicate a situation of dialogue *in praesentia*, as in *La Chute*. At most, they suggest the privileged recipient of a written narrative, without excluding a wider potential public: "That's me, folks!" (p. 112). The "last word" thus indeed creates a sensation in a narrative situation that is somewhat faked, for "folks" is not very compatible with the analytic tête-à-tête.

[8][Rimmon, "Comprehensive Theory of Narrative," p. 60.]

This precedence (I come now to the third criticism) prevents me, in any case, from accepting the correction Mieke Bal proposed regarding the use of the adjective *metadiegetic* to designate the narrative produced by an intradiegetic narrator. The disadvantage of that term is the one I drew attention to in a note on page 228: the way the prefix functions here is opposite to the way it functions in logic and linguistics, where a metalanguage is a language in which one speaks of a (second) language; in my lexicon, a metanarrative is one recounted within a narrative. To avoid this inversion, Mieke Bal proposes to substitute the term *hyponarrative*, which—fortunately, according to her—would mark the hierarchical subordination of one to the other.[9] My objection is that it marks it too much, and with an inaccurate spatial image, for if it is true that the second narrative *depends* on the first narrative, it does so, rather, in the sense of *resting on it*, as the second story of a building or the second stage of a rocket depends on the first, and so on. For me, the "hierarchy" (a word I don't much care for) of first, second, etc., levels is progressive, and I say on page 228 that every narrative is at a level "higher" than the level of the narrative on which it depends and which supports it. If I were to abandon *meta-*, therefore, it would not be in favor of *hypo-* but, quite obviously and as one might expect, in favor of *hyper-*. But that vertical representation is perhaps not the most felicitous one available, and I much prefer the inclusionary arrangement depicted a few pages earlier by my stick figures with their balloons. Its terminological paradigm could be *extradiegetic, intradiegetic, intra-intradiegetic,* etc. But *metadiegetic* seems to me certainly clear enough, and it offers the advantage—to me, an important one—of forming a system with *metalepsis*. As for the contradiction with the usage

---

[9]Bal, "The Narrating and the Focalizing," p. 247, and "Notes on Narrative Embedding," *Poetics Today* 2 (1981), 41–59. In *Narrative Fiction* (p. 92), Rimmon uses the adjective *hypodiegetic* in the same spirit.

in linguistics, I can put up with that, and apparently the linguists are not especially troubled by it. After all, *meta-* has many uses, and *metaphysics* does not mean a discourse on physics or *metathesis* a statement about a thesis (a certain amount of bad faith is not ill advised in controversy—it is one of the rules of the genre).

On pages 232–234 I proposed a typology of metadiegetic narratives according to the "main types of relationships" they maintain with the first narrative. In fact, I was dealing with types of thematic relations, but other types could be considered—for example, relations according to the mode of narration: oral (as in *The Thousand and One Nights*), written (as for *The Curious Impertinent*), plastic (as in *Moyse sauvé*). But the thematic relation itself has been subdivided a little differently (and independently of my work, with which he was not familiar) by John Barth,[10] an expert in the matter, as we already know.

I distinguished three basic types, depending on whether the second narrative, evoking the causes or antecedents of the diegetic situation in which it occurs, fulfills an explanatory function (Ulysses to the Phaeacians: "This is what brought me here"); or whether it tells a story linked to that of the diegesis by a (purely thematic) relationship of contrast or similarity, which—if perceived by the narratee—may possibly have an effect on the diegetic situation and on the sequence of events (the moral fable told by Menenius Agrippa); or whether, devoid of thematic relevance, the second narrative plays a role in the diegesis simply by virtue of the narrating act itself (Scheherazade pushing back death by dint of narratives). What interested me here, and what governed the

[10]John Barth, "Tales within Tales within Tales," *Antaeus* 43 (Autumn 1981), 45–63. Cf. Cynthia Liebow, "La Transtextualité dans *The Sot-Weed Factor* de John Barth," thesis (Ecole des Hautes Etudes en Sciences Sociales, Paris, 1982).

arrangement of my three types, was the (increasing) importance of the narrative act. What interests Barth is, in fact, the thematic relationship between the two actions. Thus, he distinguishes a first type, with no thematic relation ("So tell us a story while we're waiting for the rain to stop"); a second type, with a purely thematic relation (this is the first case of my type 2); and a third type with a "dramaturgical" relation— that is, one in which the thematic relation, perceived by the narratee, has consequences in the first action (this is the second case of my type 2). His three types, then, correspond to my second and third types, which obviously shows that he did not perceive my type 1 and that he subdivides my type 2 more sharply than I did—and in this I agree with him. It seems to me also, and finally, that he undervalues a phenomenon of which, as a good reader of *The Thousand and One Nights*, he is obviously not unaware: the (potentially paramount) diegetic function of the act of intradiegetic narrating—not only to kill time, which is already something, but also, as with Scheherazade, to gain time and thereby save one's head.

So I think that by using Barth's typology to improve mine, we can end up with a more detailed, if not complete, distribution that I would define more sharply than before in functional terms:

(1) explanatory function (by metadiegetic analepsis; this is my previous type 1);

(2) a function that neither Barth nor I thought of but that now comes to mind: the predictive function of a metadiegetic prolepsis, telling not the antecedent causes but the subsequent consequences of the diegetic situation, like Jocabel's dream about the future of Moïse in *Moyse sauvé*; this group includes all the premonitory dreams and prophetic narratives, the oracle of Oedipus, the witches of Macbeth, etc.;

(3) a purely thematic function; this is Barth's type 2 and the beginning of my ex-type 2; remember that the *mise en abyme* is only a very intensified variant of this function;

(4) a persuasive function: this is both the continuation of my ex-type 2 and Barth's type 3 ("dramaturgical");

(5) a distractive function: this is Barth's type 1;

(6) an obstructive function: this is my ex-type 3. However, we must repeat that in the last two types, the function depends not on a thematic relation between the two diegeses but on the narrating act itself, which could at one extreme be an act of completely insignificant speech, as with parliamentary filibustering or the biblical lines and verses of song that the two reporters Harry Blount and Alcide Jolivet take turns dropping off at the telegraph window at Kolyvan, each one tying up the wire to prevent the other one from sending any dispatches.[11]

Two or three voluntary self-criticisms, to finish up with narrative level. The assertion (p. 231) according to which "second-degree narrative is a form that goes back to the very origins of epic narrating, since Books IX–XII of the *Odyssey* . . . are devoted to the narrative [of] Ulysses" is even more erroneous (and, to tell the truth, completely foolish) than the assertion I have already criticized myself for about the high epic antiquity of analepses—with which it has much in common, since the Odyssean analepsis is metadiegetic. It cannot be said that the *Iliad* abounds in second narratives; even less can it be said that the *Odyssey* exhibits "the origins of epic narrating"; I see it, rather, and I have said so elsewhere, as the beginning of a transition, both formal and thematic, from the epic to the novel. The mists of time are a little more remote.

Another blunder (p. 232, and even earlier, on p. 214) con-

---

[11]Jules Verne, *Michel Strogoff*, chapter 17. We are dealing here with a borderline case. For Scheherazade, or the distracting narrative, the effect of obstruction or distraction depends on the interest of the metadiegetic content. However, we should not confuse *interest* with *thematic relationship*: the most enthralling narrative is not always the one that most closely evokes the situation in which it is told but is, for example, the one best able to "be distracting." That phrase covers (and covers very well) our types 5 and 6.

cerns *Lord Jim,* whose narrative "entanglement" I twice exaggerated. There is nothing, after all, but a first narrator, a second narrator (Marlow), and, recounted by the latter, some narratives in the third degree; that falls fairly far short of the records set by *The Thousand and One Nights* or *The Saragossa Manuscript* or the "Menelaiad." I must have displaced onto narrative structure an obscurity of another order.

But perhaps the most substantial criticism one could direct at this section on *level* would be that its very presence exaggerates the relative importance of this category with respect to the category of *person,* and the table on page 248 certainly has the defect of showing the intersection of two oppositions that are not equally interesting. Just as a scene in dialogue is narrative or dramatic depending on the mere presence or absence of some declarative statements, so the intradiegetic nature of a narrative is very often, as we see clearly in Maupassant and again in *Jean Santeuil,* only a strategem of presentation, a conventionality that, in many respects, is insignificant. And reciprocally, all that is needed to convert an extradiegetic narration into an embedded narration is a sentence of presentation (or, as in *Portnoy,* of conclusion), without any other modification. Thus:

> In a Parisian drawing room, three men were chatting in front of the fireplace. All of a sudden one of them said, "My dear Marcel, you must have led a fascinating life. Would you tell us about it?"
>
> "With pleasure," answered Marcel, "but I advise you to sit down, for it may well take some Time."
>
> While his listeners were making themselves comfortable in easy chairs, Marcel cleared his throat and began: "For a long time I used to go to bed early," etc.[12]

[12]This unpublished incipit, a mediocre pastiche of Maupassant, does *not* appear in the notebooks preserved at the Bibliothèque Nationale, N.A.Fr. 16,640–16,702 [the Proust manuscripts]. I owe my knowledge of it solely to a collector in Olivet in the department of Loiret, whose wish to remain anonymous I respect.

15 *Person (I)*

To convert "person"—that is, in fact, to change the narrator's relationship to his story (or, concretely, to change the narrator)—obviously requires a more substantial and sustained intervention, and the odds are that it will also entail more consequences. Dorrit Cohn, protesting against Wayne Booth's view that in traditional narratology the category of person has been the most "overworked" of distinctions, retorts that it has been "decidedly *under*worked" by French narratologists, and especially by the author of *Narrative Discourse*.[1] This criticism is not unfounded, although unlike other people, and particularly, as I have said, unlike the author of *Transparent Minds*, I still support the Boothian protest of overestimation. In this area it is not easy to find the right balance. Dorrit Cohn, who credits me with having somewhat rehabilitated this category "in the guise of [my] heterodiegetic and homodiegetic narrative types" (p. 163), maintains that I still devote too little attention to it and do so too late to integrate it into my other basic categories; and she, like Shlomith Rimmon[2] and Mieke Bal[3] before her, notes a regrettable ab-

[1]Cohn, "Encirclement of Narrative," p. 163.
[2]Rimmon, "Comprehensive Theory of Narrative," p. 59.
[3]Bal, *Narratologie*, pp. 112–113.

sence of "correlation with focalization." This is the main point, which I shall speak to at greater length later; for now I shall merely note that the importance of Person, in the minds of even its most determined champions, is seemingly measured by its relationship to questions of mood, which involuntarily confirms the critical importance of these latter.

I want, first, to reiterate my reservations about the term *person* itself, a term I continue to use only in deference to custom, recalling that in my view every narrative is, explicitly or not, "in the first person" since at any moment its narrator may use that pronoun to designate himself. The classical novel felt free to use it, as these three examples, chosen (as the saying goes) almost at random, testify: "*My* name is Chariton of Aphrodisias, secretary to Athenagoras the lawyer, and *my* story is all about a love affair that started in Syracuse"; "In a village of La Mancha, which *I* prefer to leave un-named, there lived not long ago one of those gentlemen . . ."; "*I* have told my Reader, in the preceding Chapter, that Mr. Allworthy inherited a large Fortune . . . ." The first example is the beginning of the earliest of all our novels, *The Adventures of Chaereas and Callirhoe;*[4] everyone has surely identified the second;[5] and the third opens Chapter III of *Tom Jones.* The general distinction between "first-person" and "third-person" narratives thus operates within this inevitably personal character of all discourse, depending on the narrator's relation (presence or absence) to the story he tells: "first person" indicates his presence as a character of whom mention is made,[6] "third person" his absence as such a character. That is what I

[4][Gareth L. Schmelling, *Chariton* (New York: Twayne Publishers, 1974), p. 81.]

[5][Norton Critical Edition.]

[6]I specify "mention," for one could imagine a story in which the narrator, implicitly present as a character, would never be mentioned because he was not playing any role. But I imagine that the first-person plural would be difficult to avoid.

denote by the more technical—but, to my mind, less ambiguous—terms of homo- and heterodiegetic narrating.

The critique of the traditional terms has been very well developed by Nomi Tamir[7] and Susan Ringler.[8] But Ringler's position is the more radical, since she holds that certain narratives, like *Portrait of the Artist,* quite simply have *no narrator.* From a generic point of view, the scope of such an assertion remains poorly defined; Ringler seems to include in it the narrative "with an omniscient narrator" of the Balzacian type and the "figural" narrative with fixed internal focalization, but both Balzac and the James of *The Ambassadors* feel free to allow the appearance of a sometimes very ponderous narrator. From a descriptive point of view, the phrase *narrative without a narrator* seems to me able to designate, very hyperbolically (for example, in Joyce and Hemingway), only the wholly relative silence of a narrator who keeps in the background as much as possible and takes care never to designate himself (and despite Flaubert's objectivist proclamations, we know that this is not the case with *Bovary*). But here hyperbole seems to me frankly excessive.

The myth of the narrative without a narrator or of the story that tells itself goes back, let us remember, at least to Percy Lubbock, whose formulations were taken up almost literally (but no doubt unwittingly) by Benveniste apropos of his category of *story (vs. discourse).* Earlier I quoted Lubbock's words;[9] I must now bring to mind Benveniste's, although everyone remembers them: "As a matter of fact, there is then no longer even a narrator. The events are set forth chronologically, as they occurred. No one speaks here; the events seem to narrate themselves."[10] As we see, Benveniste uses the mo-

---

[7]Nomi Tamir, "Personal Narrative and Its Linguistic Foundation," *PTL* 1 (1976), 403–429.

[8]Ringler, "Narrators and Narrative Contexts," pp. 158 ff.

[9]See above, Chapter 8, note 3.

[10]Benveniste, *Problèmes de linguistique générale* (Paris: Gallimard, 1966), p. 241 [*Problems in General Linguistics*, p. 208].

dal *seem* to moderate the idea that the events are telling themselves; but with respect to the absence of a narrator, he provides no qualification at all. Rarely has an unwise phrase, immediately taken literally, created more havoc. And since I contributed to popularizing the phrase in the field of poetics, I feel obligated to clarify the matter here.

In "Frontiers of Narrative," I quoted Benveniste's text and gave it my full approval: "A perfect description of what is, in its essence and in its radical opposition to any form of personal expression on the part of the speaker, narrative in the pure state . . . the complete absence . . . not only of the narrator, but also of the narration itself . . . the text is there, before our eyes, without being proffered by anyone. . . ."[11] I would no doubt have done better that day to sprain my wrist, but (failing that) I immediately added that the opposition between "narrative" and discourse was never so absolute, that neither of the two was ever found in a pure state (I showed it with the very example of *Gambara* that Benveniste had invoked), and, especially, that the opposition was not between two symmetrical terms but between a general state (discourse) and a particular state marked by exclusions or abstentions (narrative), which thus for me was only *a form of discourse* in which the marks of the enunciating were never more than provisionally and precariously suspended (I ought to have added *"and very partially,"* for ultimately any statement is in itself a trace of the enunciating; that, it seems to me, is one of the teachings of pragmatics). Since then, the myth has spread with the irresistible seductive power of extreme formulations, and we will find it, for example, as I have said, in a book by Ann Banfield,[12] where she happily holds forth with the royal self-assurance of Chomskyan linguistics.

Banfield's starting point is the sound (if not original) observation that certain characteristic forms of written narrative,

---

[11]*Figures of Literary Discourse*, pp. 138–140.
[12]Banfield, *Unspeakable Sentences*.

like the aorist (the French *passé simple*) and free indirect discourse, are by and large unknown in spoken language. From that exclusion in fact she derives an impossibility in principle: such sentences she alleges to be radically "unspeakable." That sliding is characteristic of generative grammar, always quick to declare "unacceptable" whatever has not yet been accepted. From the supposed "unspeakableness," Banfield fearlessly deduces that the texts in which such statements appear cannot be, *and therefore are not,* uttered by anyone. So no one is speaking in them, and that is why your daughter is mute, the function of communication has been eliminated, the author has "definitively disappeared from the text" (p. 222) and the narrator along with him, and language has now become "objective knowledge," "render[ing] its subjective aspects opaque" (p. 271). That metamorphosis of discourse corresponds, apparently, to the "modern division between history and consciousness, object and subject. Narration is thus that literary form which exhibits the very structure of modern thought" (p. 254). That is, narrative is contemporaneous with Cartesian thought and with Huygens's invention of the pendulum clock and the telescope:

> It is, no doubt, not accidental that it was the period in intellectual history sometimes called "cartesian" which saw the emergence in France of the sentence with an unspoken historical tense and, at the same time, in the *Fables* of La Fontaine, the sentence of represented speech and thought and that it was this same period in which the pendulum clock and the telescope were invented. (p. 273)

It is, no doubt, not accidental.

Ann Banfield quotes with some contempt (pp. 68–69) those authors (Barthes and Todorov, for example) who have affirmed, on the contrary, the impossibility of a narrative without a narrator. Nevertheless, I place myself unhesitatingly on the side of that pitiable band, since the main point of *Narrative Discourse*, beginning with its title, reflects the assumption that there is an enunciating instance—the narrating—with its narrator and its narratee, fictive or not, represented or not, silent or chatty, but always present in what is indeed for me, I fear, an act of communication. For me, therefore, the widespread affirmations (new avatar of the old "showing" and therefore of the very old *mimésis*) according to which no one in the narrative is speaking arise not only from the force of convention but also from an astonishing deafness to texts. In the most unobtrusive narrative, someone is speaking to me, is telling me a story, is inviting me to listen to it as he tells it, and this invitation—confiding or urging—constitutes an undeniable stance of narrating, and therefore of a narrator. Even the first sentence of "The Killers" (the knee-jerk representative of "objective" narrative)—"The door of Henry's lunchroom opened"—presupposes a narratee capable, among other things, of accepting the fictive familiarity of "Henry," the existence of the lunchroom, and the singleness of its door and thus, as it has so well been put, of *entering* into the fiction. Whether fiction or history, narrative is a discourse; with language, one can produce only discourse; and even in a statement as "objective" as "Water boils at 100°C" [*L'eau bout à 100 degrés*], everyone can and must hear in the use [in French] of the "notorious" article a very direct appeal to his knowledge of the watery element. Narrative without a narrator, the utterance without an uttering, seem to me pure illusion and, as such, "unfalsifiable." Who has ever refuted the existence of an illusion? I can therefore set against its devotees only this regretful confession: "Your narrative without a narrator may perhaps exist, but for the forty-seven years during which I have been reading narratives, I have never met one." *Regretful* is, moreover, a term of pure politeness, for if I were to meet such a narrative, I would flee as quickly as my legs could carry me: when I open a book, whether it is a narrative or not, I do so to have the author *speak to me*. And since I am not yet either deaf or dumb, sometimes I even happen to answer him.

The secondary distinction between the homodiegetic with a protagonist-narrator ("hero") and the homodiegetic with a witness-narrator is an old one, since we find it as early as 1955 in Friedman's article. I added to it only the term *autodiegetic* to designate the protagonist-narrator and, a little hastily, the idea that the only choice available to the narrator is between those two extreme roles. I recognize that this hypothesis has no theoretical basis and that, a priori, nothing would prevent a narrative from being taken on by a character in the story who was secondary but active. I note only that I know of no examples of it, or more exactly that the question is not put in those terms. After all, Watson, Carraway, and Zeitblom are indeed sorts of deuteragonists, or tritagonists, in the stories they tell; they do not spend all their time peeping through keyholes. But the way things happen, it is as if their role of narrator and their function—*as narrator*—of setting off the hero tended to eclipse their own behavior or, more exactly, to make it, and their own character along with it, transparent: however important their role may be at one or another moment in the story, their narrative function eclipses their diegetic function. Only the hero, who has no one in front to eclipse him, escapes the inevitable obliteration, but I would readily add: *and not necessarily*. The autobiographical hero, too, is very often in the position of observer, and the idea of *witness-hero* is perhaps not so contradictory as one might think a priori. The picaro often does more watching than participating; Des Grieux is controlled by his passion and the incomprehensible behavior of his mistress; and Marcel himself, up to the final revelation that invests him with his mission, is scarcely more than a passive hero.[13] The "first-per-

[13] I am reminded of this statement in *Degree Zero*, certainly hyperbolic but

son" novel, as fictive autobiography, is most often a novel of apprenticeship, and apprenticeship often consists mainly of looking and listening, or of licking one's wounds. (Even so, I will not say that the first person is the obligatory "voice" of a novel of apprenticeship: *Wilhelm Meister* is a fairly striking exception. Besides, at least one novel of apprenticeship exists in which the narrating is entrusted to an external witness: this is *The Way of All Flesh*. And *Doctor Faustus* is not far from that, simply pushing the apprenticeship a bit beyond its customary limits.)

I am not sure whether I would adhere today to the idea of an impassable boundary between the two types, hetero- and homodiegetic. Franz Stanzel, on the contrary and in a way I often find convincing, insists on allowing for the possibility of a progressive gradation—either with respect to "figural" (focalized) narrating (in which certain authors, like the Thackeray of *Henry Esmond*, alternate the *I* and the *he*) or with respect to the "authorial" type (in which texts like *Madame Bovary*, *Vanity Fair*, and *Karamazov*, with their fellow-townsman–contemporary–narrator, flirt very obviously with the homodiegetic type that has a witness-narrator).[14] The purest example of the latter could well be the narrator of *The Possessed*, very present but not constantly so, lacking a real role in the action, and (unlike Watson and Zeitblom) carefully kept in semi-anonymity ("It's Mr. G——v, a young man of classical education, in touch with the highest society": thus Liputin introduces him in Chapter III-9[15]). I said above that the mere presence of an epilogue in the present tense could be enough to introduce a touch of homodiegeticity, and I have no reason to go back on what I said: contrary to the present tense of commentary or of a reference solely to the

---

not devoid of all truth: "In the novel, the 'I' is usually a spectator, and . . . it is the 'he' who is the actor" (pp. 34–35). [See above, Chapter 11, note 4.]
[14]See below, Chapter 17.
[15][Modern Library Edition, trans. Constance Garnett.]

moment of narrating, this use of the present tense unequivo-
cally indicates a narrator's relationship to his story, which is a
relationship of contemporaneity. On the basis of that, one
would justifiably hesitate between diagnosing homodiegesis
or heterodiegesis—depending on the definitions of these
terms, which in themselves, after all, have nothing absolute
about them. Today, therefore, I would instead be inclined to
concede the borderline to Stanzel's gradualism, despite the
reservation of Dorrit Cohn, who alleges against it the condition of grammatical impossibility: "*No* text," she says, "can be
placed *on* the boundary separating first- and third-person narration: for the simple reason that the grammatical difference
pertaining between persons is not relative but absolute."[16]
The "reason" is incontestable, but the conclusion may or
may not be, depending on the meaning given to the word
text. It would be difficult for a *sentence* to be in both camps at
once, but a more extended text could alternate (as does *Esmond* or *La Route des Flandres*); or could be placed, like *Bovary*
or *Karamazov*, so close to the boundary that one cannot really
tell on which side it lies; or could play with the narrator's
capacities for (dis)simulation (as Borges does in "The Form of
the Sword," which I quoted on pages 246–247, or as Max
Frisch does in *Stiller*). Dorrit Cohn argues here a little too
much in terms of *grammatical person*, and I have already spoken of the indifferent reliability of that criterion. If we abandon it in favor of the opposition homodiegesis/hetero-
diegesis, we must indeed admit the possibility (and must
note the existence) of mixed or ambiguous borderline situations: that of the contemporary chronicler, some examples of
which I have just evoked, always on the verge of participa-
tion, or at least of a presence in the action that is in effect the
presence of a witness; or, more rare and more subtle, that of
the subsequent historian (the one in *Un Roi sans divertisse-*

16Cohn, "Encirclement of Narrative," p. 168.

ment) who tells of events that occurred "in his district" (geographic proximity, as with the narrator in *Karamazov*) but well before his birth (temporal distance, contrary to the *Karamazov* narrator) and that he knows about only by intermediary testimony. This is typically the situation of the first narrator of *Un Roi*, who himself admirably expresses the ambiguity of his situation: "Then they had very fine days. I say 'they'—naturally I wasn't there, since all that happened in 1843, but I have had to ask so many questions and have put myself in their shoes to get at the meaning of it that I have finally become part of it all."[17] Giono, as we know, called that narrative a *chronicle*, but to him the status of that "genre" is very open, and it encompasses equally well, besides *Un Roi sans divertissement*, an autodiegetic narrative like *Noé* or a contemporary chronicle like *Le Moulin de Pologne*. That questionable labeling—that *appellation mal contrôlée*—should not, therefore, keep us from reserving the term *chronicler* for the contemporary narrator of *Karamazov* or the *Moulin* and from proposing *historian* (fictive, of course) for the narrator of *Un Roi*. The borderline, definitely not absolute, between homo- and heterodiegesis perhaps runs between those two types, if indeed there is enough space for an imaginary line—unless it lies (not far from there) between the *Karamazov* type and the *Possessed* type. I would therefore no longer say, as I did before, "Absence is absolute, but presence has degrees." Absence also has degrees, and nothing resembles a weak absence more than a dim presence. Or more simply: at what *distance* does one begin to be absent?

Even so, I will not claim that the choice of (grammatical) person is completely independent of the narrator's diegetic situation. On the contrary, it certainly seems to me that the adoption of an *I* to designate one of the characters automat-

[17]Pléiade, p. 471.

ically and inescapably imposes the homodiegetic relationship—that is, the certainty that that character *is* the narrator—and inversely but just as rigorously, the adoption of a *he*
implies that the narrator *is not* that character.

That second assertion undoubtedly presents more difficulties than the first, for, by virtue of a tendency among readers
to confuse author and narrator, it seems to go against a sanc-
tioned and even general practice—the practice Philippe Lejeune calls "third-person autobiography."[18] I say "general"
because undoubtedly all of us in the most mundane matters
have spoken of ourselves in the third person, if only (I am not
sure why[19]) when addressing very young children, in which
case the practice often affects even our way of designating the
recipient: "And now, Sweetie is going to be a good boy: Dad-
dy will be back in five minutes." And I note further that,
perhaps because their age leads them to look on all their
interlocutors as youngsters, many old people generalize this
usage, designating themselves as "the old man" or "the
grandmother." As for literary texts, inevitably I refer to the
case of Caesar's *Commentaries* and to the examples Lejeune
cited—partial (Gide, Leiris, Barthes) or complete (Henry Adams, Norman Mailer). Texts or statements of that kind seem
to me to constitute, as Lejeune more or less says, cases of
fictive, or figural, dissociation among the authorial, narratorial, and "actorial" agents:[20] we know or guess that the
hero "is" the author, but the type of narrating that has been

[18]Philippe Lejeune, *Je est un autre* (Paris: Seuil, 1980), chapter 2.

[19]It certainly has something to do with a sort of demonstrative and ped-
agogical use of language. In the same way, we unintentionally accustom
young children to speaking of themselves in the third person, no doubt
because that form allows a statement to be transferred from one mouth to
another without a grammatical transformation: "Sweetie is a big boy, he's
eating his soup with a fork."

[20]Lejeune, "Figure d'énonciation," *Je est une autre*, p. 34. I myself said
"enallage of convention" (p. 244), which amounts to the same thing: the
enallage of *I* into *he* is certainly a figure of enunciating.

adopted pretends that the narrator is not the hero. For that reason, we ought to speak here of *heterodiegetic autobiography*,[21] although that expression (like Lejeune's, except that his was less blunt) does violence—a violence Lejeune himself has taken full responsibility for—to the Lejeunean definition of autobiography: an identity of the three agents, author, narrator, and hero.

That figural dissociation, it seems to me, calls for two (that is, three) possible readings: either (the reader perceives that) the author, speaking manifestly about himself, pretends to be speaking about someone else (Stendhal evoking "Dominique" or "Salviati," Gide evoking "Fabrice" or "X"); or (he perceives that) the author, still speaking manifestly about himself, pretends that someone else is speaking about him (Gide giving the floor here and there to an imaginary biographer named Edouard, and—much more dramatically—Gertrude Stein pretending to let Alice Toklas write Stein's own biography). In the first case, the author is indistinguishable from the narrator, and the character is fictively dissociated; in the second case, the author (the person whose name goes on the text) is indistinguishable from the character (this book signed "Gertrude Stein" tells the life of Gertrude Stein), and the narrator (Toklas) is fictively dissociated. But in both cases the narrator is dissociated from the character, and because of that the narrating is heterodiegetic. Finally, in particular when the various agents are not (all) named and thereby dramatized,

[21]The *Gil Blas* type of novel is obviously and systematically an autodiegetic heterobiography. Fictive, in that case, but others exist that are more tied to historical or personal reality: *Robinson Crusoe* is a little (very little), and despite the change in name, a biography of Selkirk, and the pseudo-biographies of real people of the type *Memoirs of Monsieur d'Artagnan* (by Courtilz de Sandras), *Mémoires d'Hadrien* (by Marguerite Yourcenar), or *L'Allée du roi* (the pseudo-memoirs of Mme de Maintenon by Françoise Chandernagor) are indeed the exact counterpart, in the category of "referential" narrative, of *The Education of Henry Adams*.

the reader may justifiably hesitate between those two inter-pretations—that is, between the two possible points of dis-sociation. In my view this is the case with the heterodiegetic pages of *Roland Barthes par Roland Barthes,* where one hardly knows whether (going back to the terms Lejeune used about Leiris[22]) one should believe that the author, who is presumed to be speaking about himself, is pretending to speak about someone else (like Balzac describing himself under cover of the features of Marcas or Savarus) or is pretending that some-one else is speaking about him (like Gertrude Stein via Alice Toklas). That constitutive indefiniteness must obviously be respected and maintained. Moreover, it seems to me to be equally present in general usage: in "Sweetie fell" (through the fifth-floor window) it is very hard to say whether Sweetie-speaker, taking on the narrative, is objectifying Sweetie-acro-bat, or whether, taking on the acrobat, he is objectifying the narrator by doing a pastiche of the language of others. Sweet-ie, questioned on this point, declines to consider this prob-lem; a three-year-old's willingness to oblige has its limits. The same uncertainty when Sweetie's great-grandfather declares, "The old man, he's getting old."

[22]Lejeune, *Je est un autre*, p. 34.

16 *Person (II)*

Dorrit Cohn suggests that my "Proustian paradigm" led me to pay more attention to the homodiegetic system than to the heterodiegetic one.[1] The explanation is plausible, but I am not sure the observation is correct. In fact, of the eight pages I devote to "person" in the Proustian narrative, more than half of them bear not on its (final) homodiegetic nature but on the transition Proust made from the third person of *Jean Santeuil* to the first person of the *Recherche*, thus accepting in advance Dorrit Cohn's good advice: "Obviously, one must continually go back and forth across the border to become aware of regional differences and particularities."

I exaggerate, of course, since, in pursuit of Proust, I took the trip in only one direction. But I have read narratives in the third person and I have mentally done a little rapid commuting from one system to the other, straddling the frontier like Chaplin at the end of I don't know which film. I have even contemplated some real or imaginary exercises of *transvocalization*, or rewriting from first to third person and vice versa.[2] Be that as it may, Dorrit Cohn herself very successfully completes my one trip with some examples of the reverse conver-

---

[1]Cohn, "Encirclement of Narrative," p. 163.
[2]*Palimpsestes*, pp. 335–339.

sion—the crossing (which is apparently more frequent) from first person to third: Dostoevski's for *Crime and Punishment*, James's for *The Ambassadors*, Kafka's for *The Castle*.[3] These four examples (counting Proust's) are undoubted proof of a motivated decision to make a narrative conversion—and are therefore proof that these authors felt one system or the other to be superior (or at least to have a circumstantial advantage)—and are therefore definitely proof that the authors felt the question to be relevant. (Of course, here one can challenge my presupposition of a transvocalizing rewriting from *Santeuil* to the *Recherche*, which could be looked on as two wholly distinct works—an interesting controversy. Nevertheless the author, in passing from one to the other, made a narrative conversion; and we could, no doubt, find more substantial examples of authors who, in the course of their careers, passed from one predilection to the other. Roughly speaking, that is the case with Hammett, who passed from the first person to the third.)

I am not sure, however, that from these examples one can derive a very clear idea of the response—that is, of the exact advantage gained by each of these conversions. Readings among the variants and the sundry early drafts can induce skepticism toward the prevailing (and somewhat too sanguine) idea that the final state is generally superior—such a valuation originating with the well-known concept of retrospective motivation. Dostoevski's (narrative) conversion is apparently accompanied by no commentary and has left no

---

[3][For Kafka, see] Cohn, *Transparent Minds*, pp. 169–171. Stanzel ("Teller-Characters") mentions as examples the case of Jane Austen for *Sense and Sensibility* and that of Joyce Cary for *Prisoner of Grace*; Jacques Petit ("Une Relecture de Mauriac . . . ," *Edition et interprétation des manuscrits littéraires* [Bern, 1981]) mentions two more cases, both in Mauriac, *Le Désert de l'amour* and *Le Baiser au lépreux*. In the other direction (Proust's), we know of the conversion Gottfried Keller made, consolidating in the first person the whole of *Green Henry* twenty-five years after its first publication.

trace of the first version. James's conversions for *Maisie* and *The Ambassadors* are vouched for only by the later testimony of the prefaces. The difficulty James evoked for *Maisie* is clear enough (the little girl's limited vocabulary) but not very convincing (Maisie could have told the story many years later). As for *The Ambassadors*, James's commentary is as vague as it is vehement: he seems to see in the homodiegetic temptation a "gulf" from which he escaped, "the darkest abyss of romance" (those old bachelors always exaggerate the little that goes on in their lives). Of these examples, the only one that allows us to make a comparison is the conversion of *The Castle*, and Dorrit Cohn's commentary certainly illustrates the ambiguity of the case. She shows full well the easiness of the transformation (simple substitution of pronouns) and the modal equivalence between the initial autodiegetic drafting and the final focalized, heterodiegetic version; then, struck by a misgiving about her argument, she adds, "It would be a grave error, however, to take the case of *The Castle* as proof of the unimportance of grammatical person for the structure and meaning of a narrative" (p. 171). One therefore expects to see here an account of the advantages of Kafka's final decision; but Cohn immediately takes refuge in the circular argument of the infallibility of the author's choice: "Kafka would surely not have bothered to make this laborious change in midstream had he thought that it was of no consequence to his fiction." One could pretty much argue the other way— "Kafka would surely not have bothered to make this change in midstream if he had expected it to entail substantial modifications"—without mentioning that, after all, Kafka's final decision ("kindly burn everything") does not exactly encourage one to approve of all his choices. Be that as it may, here we are caught in a circle from which Dorrit Cohn, like anybody and everybody, can break free only with a conjecture: "*More or less* consciously he *must have known* that there were advantages to the K. over the I, and the drawbacks of the retrospective techniques for rendering consciousness *may have* had *a* share in his decision" (I italicize the phrases that express doubt or evasion). Indeed, the appeal is always the same: it is Lubbock's description of the "drawbacks" entailed in the (necessarily?) "retrospective" nature of first-person narrative.[4]

I confess that all these a priori descriptions and a posteriori justifications leave me skeptical. The modal consequences (for, once again, that is essentially what we are dealing with) of the narrative choice seem to me neither as substantial nor, especially, as mechanical as they are often said to be. Dorrit Cohn herself has shown, using the example of *Hunger* by Knut Hamsun, that a "retrospective" homodiegetic narrative could be as rigorously focalized on the hero as a "figural" narrative, and Proust demonstrates the same thing on many pages of the *Recherche*. So I am not totally convinced that a rewriting of *Crime and Punishment, The Ambassadors,* or *The Castle* into the first person would be such a catastrophe (an arduous and unpleasant task, certainly, but far be it from me to think of sentencing anyone to doing it). Inversely, the reason—also wholly conjectural—that I give for Proust's final choice (the need to assign the ideological investment of the *Recherche* to the narrator's discourse) can seem very flimsy. In that respect, the "third person" apparently did not unduly restrain, for example, Mann, or Broch, or Musil.

My various experiences, real or imaginary, in transvocalizing have convinced me of five things: (1) the versatility of the vocalic positions makes them roughly equivalent to one another from the point of view of modal consequences; (2) the only consequence that, in principle, is inevitable—namely, the impossibility of focalizing through one character after vocalizing (and thus prefocalizing) through another—can be cir-

[4]Lubbock, *The Craft of Fiction,* pp. 144–145; see, more recently, Mendilow (referred to on p. 168 of *Narrative Discourse*).

cumvented by paraleptic infractions handled more or less skillfully; (3) as James, Lubbock, et al. have seen, hetero-diegetic narrating is thus *able*, naturally and without any transgression, to do more than homodiegetic narrating can do; (4) *but* an artist may always, as we know, prefer the stimulating drawbacks of constraint to the sedative virtues of freedom; (5) finally, the importance of the vocalic choice could well derive not from any modal or temporal kind of advantage or drawback but simply from the hard fact of its existence: the writer, I imagine, one day *wants* to write this narrative in the first person and that narrative in the third person, for no reason at all, just for a change. Some writers are totally resistant to one or the other, for no reason at all, because it is what it is, because they are what they are: why do some writers use black ink and others blue ink? (That will be the subject of another study.) The reader, in turn, receives thus-and-such a narrative equipped with its vocalic position, which seems to him as indissociable from it as their color is from the eyes he loves[5]—their color that, in the absence of a counter-proof, he thinks is better suited to them than any other would be. In short, the most profound (the least *conditional*) reason here, as is often the case elsewhere, is "because that's the way it is." Everything else is motivation.

[5]For example, Gilberte's, of whose blueness Marcel is enamored only because they are black (Proust, *Recherche*, P I, 141 [RH I, 153]).

17 *Narrative Situations*

That reservation about the supposed influence of voice over mood is not enough to dismiss the question (left in abeyance) of considering them jointly in the guise of what is customarily called a "narrative situation." That complex term was proposed more than a quarter of a century ago by Franz Stanzel, who since then has persisted in deepening and revising the classification he proposed for it in 1955. Dorrit Cohn is quite right to reproach both me and the whole of "French narratology" for slighting the contribution made by that important literary theorist,[1] and certainly an attentive reading of his first book would have spared us, in the 1960s, some belated "discoveries." This is not the place for an exposition that would certainly not be superfluous on the banks of the Seine but that has already been given elsewhere, and remarkably well, by Dorrit Cohn—and in a way that closely concerns me, since her review of the *Theorie des Erzählens* partly proceeds by comparing that work with "Discours du récit." I refer the reader, therefore, to her very solid article and, of course, to Stanzel's two main books, which are readily available in [English] translation.

[1]Cohn, "Encirclement of Narrative," pp. 158–160. It is obviously this article that I refer to throughout the chapter.

As Dorrit Cohn says and very clearly shows, the essential difference between our two ways of proceeding is that Stanzel's is "synthetic" whereas mine (as I claim on several occasions) is analytic.[2] "Synthetic" is perhaps a little deceptive, for it leads one to expect Stanzel to synthesize elements he will first have isolated and studied, each for its own sake. Just the opposite is true. In 1955, Stanzel was starting from the general intuition of a certain number of complex facts (but already that way of referring to them is mine), which he called "narrative situations": the *authorial* (which I can only describe by analyzing it, in my terms, as nonfocalized heterodiegetic narrating—for example, *Tom Jones*); the *personal*, later rechristened *figural* (heterodiegetic with internal focalization—for example, *The Ambassadors*); and the *first-person* (homodiegetic—for example, *Moby Dick*). "Syncretic" would thus be a better term, if it did not have something of a pejorative connotation. The fact is simply that Stanzel takes as his point of departure the indisputable empirical observation that the great majority of literary narratives are divided among those three situations that he rightly calls "typical." It is only afterward, and especially in his latest book, that he attempts to analyze the situations according to three elementary, or fundamental, categories that he calls *person* (first or third), *mode* (this is more or less, according to Dorrit Cohn, what I call "distance"—the dominance of the narrator or, to use James's term, of a "reflector"), and *perspective* (which is what I call it also, but Stanzel reduces it to an opposition between

[2]The other differences noted by Cohn are my constant recourse to Proustian narrative, whereas Stanzel places himself at once in relation to general theory; his constant search for a gradation, represented by his circular diagrams, in contrast to my tables with their watertight compartments; his indifference to questions of level (his system, Cohn says, is "uni-diegetic"); and, of course, the fact that he pays no attention to questions of temporality.

internal and external so that in fact external focalization comes down to zero focalization[3]).

I will not follow Dorrit Cohn in her very detailed exposition of the advantages and drawbacks of that trio of categories, the third of which seems to her superfluous; for me, of course, the superfluous one is, instead, the second, both because I have long viewed the idea of distance (*diégésis*/*mimésis*) with suspicion and because the specification Stanzel gives it (narrator/reflector) seems to me easily reducible to our common category of perspective. Nor will I follow her in the circular labyrinth constituted, in the grand Germanic tradition (Goethe-Petersen), by the marvelous rose window Stanzel uses for representing the gradation of narrative situations and the crisscross of axes, borders, hubs, spokes, cardinal points, rims, and casings that put in concrete form the latest state (to date) of his system.[4] I have spoken elsewhere of my ambiguous response to this type of make-believe, which here is the occasion for (among other things) stimulating antitheses and pairings as fruitful as they are unexpected. Dorrit Cohn speaks in this connection of an "encirclement" of narrative; I who am sometimes accused of putting narrative into boxes or behind grids shall be the last person to condemn that way of surveying one's field, which is as good a way as any other. Besides, Stanzel's chief merit lies not in those totalizing representations but in the details of his "analyses"— that is, his readings. Like every self-respecting literary theorist, Stanzel is first a critic. But obviously that aspect of his work is not the one that can detain us here.

All the complexity (and sometimes the inextricableness) of

---

[3]In 1955, under the term *neutral* narration, Stanzel attached external focalization to his "personal" type. Since 1964, he seems to have totally dropped this category.

[4]*Theorie des Erzählens* (Göttingen: Vandenhoeck & Ruprecht, 1979), p. 334 [tr. *A Theory of Narrative*, trans. Charlotte Goedsche (Cambridge: Cambridge University Press, 1984), p. 185]; Cohn, p. 162.

his latest system is due to his desire to account for the three "narrative situations" by the overlapping of three analytic categories (here, too, the trinitarian obsession is up to its old tricks). For a combinative mind, the intersection of two oppositions of person by two oppositions of mode by two oppositions of perspective ought to produce a table of eight complex situations. But Stanzel's circular representation and his diametrical overlappings lead him to a division into *six* basic sectors—a division that can be represented as follows (I want to make clear that this circle is my simplified version and appears nowhere in his work). Between the three initial "typical" situations we see three intermediary forms, and they, too, are highly canonical: interior monologue, free indirect discourse, and "peripheral" narration. Aside from the third one, which basically comes down to the situation of the "I-witness," these buffer states seem to me hard to accept in a table of narrative situations, since the first two are, rather, ways of presenting the speech of characters.

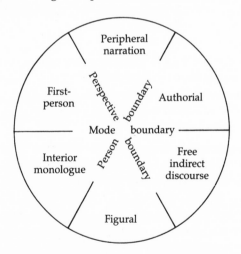

Dorrit Cohn is also not very satisfied with that six-part division. So, arguing from a sentence in which Stanzel himself recognizes "a close correspondence between internal *perspective* and the *mode* of representation dominated by the narrator," she proposes to suppress the unnecessary category of perspective. At one fell swoop that reduces the system to an intersection of two oppositions: person and mode. Whence this new circular table:

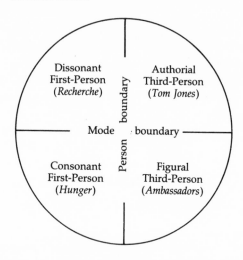

The terms *dissonant* and *consonant* are introduced here by Dorrit Cohn, who had already used them in *Transparent Minds*, but they are indeed equivalents of Stanzel's terms *authorial* (dominance of the narrator) and *figural* (dominance of the character as "reflector" or focus of the narrating). The examples proposed here in parentheses are, for the right half, Stanzel's and, for the left half, Cohn's (in *Transparent Minds*). I would gladly substitute, for obvious reasons and as Alain Bony did in his French translation of Cohn's book, the term *narratorial* (borrowed from Roy Pascal) for *authorial*. Having thus begun to amend, in turn, Cohn's amendment of Stanzel, I propose to present it in the form—which for me is now inevitable—of this double-entry table:

Person / Mode	1st	3rd
Narratorial	A *Recherche*	B *Tom Jones*
Figural	C *Hunger*	D *The Ambassadors*

This patched-up compromise, via Dorrit Cohn, between Stanzel's typology and what could be the beginning of my own will allow me to note a certain quantitative progression, starting with the three typical situations of Stanzel-1955. Cohn, who with good reason rejects the six far-too-heterogeneous types of Stanzel-1979, turns back to the past, but not entirely so, since she expands the three initial types (B, D, A + C) by one, separating C from A. We can deem this addition a step forward if we consider that it opportunely and effectively diversifies an initial typology that was a little primitive and altogether too limited to the most frequent situations. We can also deem the progress insufficient and wish for a new enlargement (with or without emendation) of the table. Now is perhaps the time to recall the other typologies mentioned in *Narrative Discourse* (pp. 185–188), which—sometimes legitimately—made room for types not represented here. Thus, Brooks and Warren, taking into account a mode of focalization more external than those envisaged by Stanzel, made one place for the *I-witness* type and another for "objective" narration à la Hemingway, which Romberg, for his part, added to the Stanzelian trio as a fourth type.[5]

[5]It is obviously the supplementary "neutral" type of Stanzel-1955. Friedman's eight types, reduced to seven in a later version (*Form and Meaning in Fiction* [Athens: University of Georgia Press, 1975], chapter 8), easily come down to this fourfold division if one disregards the secondary distinctions among what could, it seems to me, legitimately be considered subtypes.

So we see that the aforementioned trio has undergone two successive modifications, first by Romberg, who adds one type (in my terms, heterodiegetic narrating with external focalization), and then by Dorrit Cohn, who adds another (in my terms, homodiegetic narrating with internal focalization). It would indeed be tempting (and, as we all know, everything should be resisted save temptation) to add on those two additions, which would give us a list of *five* types.

That is precisely, albeit implicitly, the point reached— along another route, it is true (besides, he could not have known Dorrit Cohn's latest proposal)—by the latest to date of the typologists of narrative situations, Jaap Lintvelt.[6] First he establishes a dichotomy—that of person—which he names hetero-/homodiegetic *narrating.* Then he establishes a tripartition of *narrative types,* according to the "center of orientation" of the reader's attention, which is a sort of synthesis of my focalizations and the modes according to Stanzel: *authorial* type ($\equiv$ zero focalization), *actorial* type ($\equiv$ internal focalization), *neutral* type ($\equiv$ external focalization: this is the neutral subtype of Stanzel-1955, now making a reappearance). For Lintvelt these two distinctions are the object of separate tables that seem oblivious of each other and are never brought together in a synthesis.[7] So once more I will intervene with an amendment that will again take the form of a double-entry table, in which the two "narratings" and the three "narrative types" intersect and in which I introduce as of now, to gain time (space), the examples inherited from tradition (Stanzel, Romberg, Cohn) plus, in parentheses, the approximate equivalences between Lintvelt's terms and mine:

[6]Lintvelt, *Essai,* part 2, "Pour une typologie du discours narratif."
[7]Lintvelt, *Essai,*p. 39.

Type (Focal.) / Narrating (Relation)	Authorial (Zero focal.)	Actorial (Internal focal.)	Neutral (External focal.)
Heterodiegetic	A *Tom Jones*	B *The Ambassadors*	C "The Killers"
Homodiegetic	D *Moby Dick*	E *Hunger*	

In this factitious table one can clearly see the original trio (boxes A, B, D + E); the Cohn addition (box E); and, confirming the Romberg addition, the Lintvelt addition (box C). One can also see, I hope, where I want to end up: in this table there is one empty box, where a sixth situation—that of a neutral-homodiegetic narrating—could be accommodated. That sixth type Lintvelt evokes only to reject, considering "that such a theoretical structure would go against the real possibilities of narrative types."[8] Such an abstention may seem the soul of wisdom, but I wonder whether there is not even more wisdom (a very different kind, to be sure) in this principle of Borges's: "It is enough that a book be possible for it to exist."[9] If we adopt that optimistic view, even if only for its power of encouragement, the book in question (a narrative of the sixth type) must indeed exist somewhere on the shelves of the Library of Babel.

So I sought it there (that library is distinctly more accessible, in winter, than the Pound Library to which my respects have already been paid, and more hospitable than our wretched Bibliothèque Nationale for—how shall I say it—

[8]Lintvelt, *Essai*, p. 84.
[9]Borges, "The Library of Babel," *Fictions* (London: Calder & Boyars, 1974), p. 78.

digging in the stacks) and I found it there, several copies of it. For example, there are the first-person novels of Hammett (without counting numerous novellas) and a vast posterity in the genre of the thriller. There is also, contemporaneous with *Red Harvest* (1929), Benjy's monologue in *The Sound and the Fury*.[10] There is in addition, it seems to me, Camus's *L'Etranger*.

Those words are undoubtedly spoken a little too quickly and call for some shading or elaboration. First, of course, that characterization of *L'Etranger*, which on the whole I take from Claude-Edmonde Magny,[11] is rejected by Lintvelt. On the basis of B. T. Fitch's analyses, he assigns this novel partly to his authorial type and partly to his actorial type.[12] And indeed it is very obvious that in Camus as in Hammett[13] or

---

[10]See John Pier, "L'Instance narrative du récit à la première personne," Ph.D. diss. (New York University, 1983), chapter 3.

[11]Claude-Edmonde Magny, *L'Age du roman américain,* pp. 50–54 for Hammett and, for *L'Etranger* and a comparison with Hammett and Cain, pp. 74–76. Everything from those pages should be quoted, but to stick to the main point: "The artful filtering Camus sets up consists of presenting a hero who says *I* reporting to us only what a third person could say about him. . . . The technical paradox of Camus's narration is that it is falsely introspective . . . as is the narration of the narrator in *Red Harvest*, who gives us as impartial a report of his actions as possible. . . . The effect achieved in *Red Harvest* is not noticeably different from the effect in *The Maltese Falcon*, where the narrative unfolds in the third person." It is true that here Magny herself is relying without saying so on Sartre's article "Explication de *L'Etranger*" [tr. "Camus's 'The Outsider'" (see note 16 below)] published in 1943, which reported and partly justified this anonymous witticism: "Kafka written by Hemingway." The "technical paradox" described here is obviously that of an external focalization in the first person.

[12]See Lintvelt, *Essai,* pp. 84–88. But neither Fitch nor Lintvelt mentions Magny, of whose position they seem unaware.

[13]Thus, in *Red Harvest:* "I would rather have been cold sober, but I wasn't. If the night held more work for me I didn't want to go to it with alcohol dying in me. The snifter revived me a lot" [*The Novels of Dashiell Hammett* (New York: Alfred A. Knopf, 1965), chapter 5, p. 28]. Chapter 21 is even devoted to the narrative of a dream. Nevertheless, the overall tone is that of a hard-

Chandler, the behaviorist course is somewhat strained—for example, at the end of the first part (the knee-jerk example for psychologically oriented Camus critics), where Meursault allows himself a few words of explanation or symbolic interpretation.

The second elaboration could be formulated in the terms used by Lintvelt himself, who defines his narrative types according to what he calls the "perceptual-psychic" level. Here that pair would benefit from being separated into a perceptual level and a psychic level (this naive distinction will amuse philosophers, but everybody has to have some fun). The narrative mode of *L'Etranger* is "objective" on the "psychic" level, in the sense that the hero-narrator does not mention his thoughts (if any). It is not "objective" on the perceptual level, for we cannot say that Meursault is seen "from the outside," and even more, the external world and the other characters appear only insofar as (and to the extent that) they enter into his field of perception. The same thing, and doubtless even more systematically, in *The Sound and the Fury*:

> They held me. It was hot on my chin and on my shirt. "Drink," Quentin said. They held my head. It was hot inside me, and I began again. I was crying now, and something was happening inside me and I cried more, and they held me until it stopped happening. Then I hushed. It was still going around, and then the shapes began. . . .[14]

---

boiled hero-narrator whom modesty or contempt for all psychology generally turns away from all confidences or introspection—not to mention that a detective story, even one of this kind, must necessarily hide a portion of the detective's thoughts. The reasons for Meursault's muteness—if there are any—are obviously quite different.

[14][Modern Library Edition, p. 25.] Here Benjy *perceives* a warmth on him, then in him, but he is unable to "think" (interpret) that he is being forced to drink. This narrative position, as we know, is motivated by the fact that here the narrative is taken on by an "idiot." But Hammett's hero is certainly not an idiot, and in his case the implicit motivation, as I have mentioned, is totally different. Where between the two should Meursault go?

In this sense, of course, the mode of *Red Harvest, The Sound and the Fury*, and *L'Etranger* is, rather, internal focalization, and the most accurate overall way of putting it would perhaps be something like "internal focalization with an almost total paralipsis of thoughts."[15] Most accurate, but extremely cumbersome, like describing F major as "C major with systematic flatting of the B." Cumbersome and, above all, tendentious, for that way of putting it arbitrarily supposes that Meursault is thinking something. The inverse supposition, which would simplify everything—this is somewhat the supposition Sartre makes, holding that we see everything seen through that window pane that is Meursault's consciousness, except that "it is so constructed as to be transparent to things and opaque to meanings"[16]—seems to me equally arbitrary. So let us decline to make any interpretation and let us leave that narrative to its uncertainty, the formula for which would be, instead, "Meursault tells what he does and describes what he perceives, but he does not say (not: *what he thinks about it,* but:) *whether he thinks about it.*" That "situation," or rather, here, that narrative *stance*, is for the moment the one that best, or least badly, resembles a homodiegetic narrating that is "neutral," or in external focalization.

I do indeed say "for the moment"—that is, within the field of the literature existing at this date (and to my knowledge). But all that that is, is a given of fact; it does not answer the loftier (more "theoretical") question: is a homodiegetic narrating with rigorous external focalization *possible*?

[15]Unlike *Roger Ackroyd*, where the paralipsis—although fundamental—is very partial.

[16]J.-P. Sartre, *Situations I* (Paris: Gallimard, 1947), p. 115 [tr. "Camus's 'The Outsider,'" *Literary and Philosophical Essays*, trans. Annette Michelson (New York: Criterion Books, 1955), p. 36]. But Sartre's formulation remains ambiguous because it does not say which side of the pane Meursault is on—or, to drop the metaphor, whether the opacity of his "consciousness" of meanings is a matter of reception or transmission.

Although such a narrative would be taken on by the hero,[17] it should obviously adopt toward him, and toward everything, the point of view of an (anonymous) external observer incapable not only of knowing the hero's thoughts but also of taking on his perceptual field. Such a narrative stance is generally, not to say unanimously, considered incompatible with the logical-semantic norms of narrative discourse. That is obviously why Roland Barthes claimed that a sentence like "The tinkling of the ice cubes against the glass seemed to awaken in Bond a sudden inspiration" could not be translated into the first person.[18] A sentence like "The tinkling of the ice cubes against the glass seemed to awaken in *me* a sudden inspiration" will therefore be called impossible, or more exactly and in Chomskyan terms, "unacceptable."[19] But it seems to *me* that these edicts of unacceptability should not be overworked. At a colloquium held at Johns Hopkins in October 1966, Roland Barthes, dealing with the same example, asserted more categorically or more imprudently, "We *cannot* say, 'The tinkling of the ice seemed to give me a sudden inspiration,'" and, a little later, "I *can't* say 'I am dead.'" Jacques Derrida very quickly countered with the "I am dead" of Mr. Valdemar in Edgar Allan Poe and with the complexity of the problem of logical impossibilities in language.[20] From

[17]Or by the "witness," in a case of "peripheral" narrative. We would then have Zeitblom telling about himself as seen from the outside in the act of seeing Leverkühn from the outside. Not easy, but we don't want to discourage anyone.

[18]Barthes, "Introduction to the Structural Analysis of Narratives," p. 112.

[19]Ringler, "Narrators and Narrative Contexts," p. 176. I spoke more prudently (p. 194) about "semantic incongruity."

[20]Richard Macksey and Eugenio Donato, *The Structuralist Controversy* (Baltimore: Johns Hopkins University Press, 1970), pp. 140, 143, 155–156. Barthes took that objection into account when, some years later, he analyzed "The Facts in the Case of M. Valdemar" ("Analyse textuelle d'un conte d'Edgar Poe," in Claude Chabrol et al., *Sémiotique narrative et textuelle* [Paris: Larousse, 1973]).

the point of view we are concerned with here, the objection was perhaps not radical enough. For the question is not so much *in what sense* such propositions are "absurd" (a logical problem)[21] but (1) is it *possible* to utter propositions that are absurd (in any sense whatsoever)—a question, I venture to say, that is *literary* and the answer to which is obviously positive (witness, among others and on two occasions, Barthes's sentence itself, to which the radical objection would have been, more bluntly, perhaps, "You have just said it")—and (2) are such utterances, for the reader or the listener, in one way or another (which we should not be too quick to call "figurative"), acceptable, despite—or rather *taking into account* and thus, in a sense, *by virtue of*—their present anomalousness. What the "linguistic feeling," always one sentence behind, rejects today, it could indeed accept tomorrow under the pressure of stylistic innovation. And after all, and to come back to our (still) illusive homodiegetic narrating with external focalization, ordinary language accepts and uses every day (occasions are certainly not wanting) utterances such as "I seemed like a jerk." Thus, in my view it would be an unnecessary affront to the future to exclude that form from the "real possibilities of narrative types."[22] Cézanne, Debussy, Joyce are full of features that Ingres, Berlioz, and Flau-

[21]The two examples proposed by Barthes are obviously not absurd in the same sense. Taken literally, "I am dead" is simply *false*, like any proposition for which the uttering contradicts the utterance. It incurs the objection, "If what you say were true, you would not be able to say it." "I seemed . . ." must deal, rather, with the objection "What do you know about it?" But from a narratological point of view, the difference can be disregarded: *to be dead* and *to seem* are two states that by definition can be perceived only from without. What, moreover, is being dead, if not *seeming dead* to a spectator?

[22]Gerald Prince ("Narrative Analysis and Narratology," p. 183) gives as an example of a narrative type not yet achieved, and perhaps destined never to be, "a novel in the third person, for instance, in diary form, using the future tense, and presenting events in a nonchronological order." That is what I call a challenge, and if I had the time . . .

bert would undoubtedly have declared "unacceptable"—and so on. No one knows where the "possibilities," real or theoretical, end, with respect to anything. So it seems to me wise to "anticipate," that is, to outline a box for the type that interests us, even if for the moment *L'Etranger* fills it only provisionally and with a question mark. The kind reader is herewith requested to go and write it in himself.

So here we are, having gone from the three "typical situations" of Stanzel-1955 to six situations that certainly are not all equally widespread but that do all correspond to some combinatory potential of a table of "narrative possibilities" that, for the moment, includes only two categories, "person" and perspective. One could envisage a very much more complex table, taking into account narrative level, temporal position (subsequent, previous, or simultaneous narrating), "distance" if one is keen for that, and, in addition, parameters of order, speed, and frequency. Pushed to that point, the table could obviously no longer apply to entire works (besides, in all strictness none can do that), but only to one or another segment, sometimes very brief, since only *relation* ("person") governs in a more or less uniform way the whole of a narrative. Moreover, the table would become very difficult to represent on one page of a book. Here, therefore, for the sake of the example and by cheating a little with the resources of two-dimensional space, I will simply show the intersection in a single table of the three parameters of focalization, relation, and level. I retain the examples that have become traditional, but I reinstate the elements of my terminology. The left half is identical to the preceding table, with *L'Etranger* now taking its proper place with the question mark that befits it. The right half takes the same six types in a situation of intradiegetic narrating, and thus of metadiegetic narrative. I insert three more or less typical examples and leave three boxes empty, half from laziness and half in tribute to the reader's sagacity:

	Extradiegetic			Intradiegetic		
Level → / Focalization → / Relation →	0	Internal	External	0	Internal	External
Heterodiegetic	Tom Jones	Portrait of the Artist	"The Killers"	The Curious Impertinent	L'Ambitieux par amour	
Homodiegetic	Gil Blas	Hunger	L'Etranger?		Manon Lescaut	

it should not be too hard to find an example of a homo-metadiegetic narrative that is not (or not much) focalized. The column on the far right is more perplexing, for there one would have to unite two narrative stances that historically have not been very compatible, at least until now: the meta-diegetic, which is a "classical" feature (I mean a baroque one, from the *Odyssey* to *Lord Jim*), and external focalization, which is a "modern" feature, from Hemingway to Robbe-Grillet. But we should be able to count on the syncretic capacities (which backbiters will call the eclecticism) of "postmodern" fiction, to which that column rightfully belongs, on condition that it fill it as quickly as possible, if it still has the strength.

This proposition will not, I hope, be taken too literally. For me, what is important about it is not this or that actual combination but the combinatorial principle itself, whose chief merit is to place the various categories in an open relationship with no a priori constraints: neither unilateral *determination* in the Hjelmslevian sense ("such a choice of voice entails such a course as to mode," etc.) nor *interdependence* ("such a choice of voice and such a choice of mode reciprocally govern each other"), but simply *constellations* in which every parameter can a priori come into play with every other—on condition that the literary theorist note here and there the (s)elective affinities, the more or less broad technical or historical compatibilities, without being in too much of a hurry to proclaim definitive incompatibilities. Every day Nature and Culture breed thousands of "monsters" that are as fit as fiddles.

18   *The Narratee*

I went over the *functions of the narrator* (pp. 255–259) a little quickly. It is true that by distinguishing a *narrative* function, the study of which, logically speaking, merges with everything that preceded, and four *extranarrative* functions, the study of which, still speaking logically, has no place in a work on narrative discourse, I was and am excused from saying anymore about them. There is nothing like logic.

Let me proceed briefly here, nevertheless, to make explicit what is, besides, self-evident. The extranarrative functions are more active in the "narratorial" (that is, in our terms, the nonfocalized) type. Rigorous focalization, whether it be internal (as in *Portrait of the Artist*) or external (as in Hemingway), excludes on principle every kind of intervention by the narrator, who limits himself to recounting, pretending even to let the story (according to the old formula) "tell itself"; the use of commentarial discourse is somewhat the privilege of the "omniscient" narrator. As for the function I called "testimonial," for obvious reasons it has hardly any place except in homodiegetic narrating—of which the variant called "I-witness" is, as its name indicates, nothing but one vast attestation: "I was there, this is how it all happened." But perhaps we should also see the testimonial function operating in the types of fiction in which the narrator claims to be a chronicler or historian—that is, a retrospective witness—as in *Karamazor* or the first narrative of *Un Roi sans divertissement*. There the narrator, like every good historian, must at least attest to the truthfulness of his sources, or intermediary witnesses: "I was not there, but it all happened a century ago in my village, and this is what oral tradition says about it. . . ."[1]

Definitely too hasty was the section on the *narratee*, which Gerald Prince's article "Introduction à l'étude du narrataire" very quickly and felicitously completed. I would willingly and unashamedly annex that article, with three reservations. The first is that Prince's article is indeed still an introduction, itself hasty and sometimes disorganized. The second is that, for lack of a clear distinction between intradiegetic narratees (M. de Renoncour in *Manon Lescaut*[2]) and extradiegetic narratees (the narratee of *Père Goriot*), the necessary dissociation between narratee and reader is handled fairly roughly.

For the extradiegetic narratee is not, as the intradiegetic narratee is, a "relay point" between the narrator and the implied reader. He merges totally with this implied reader, who is in turn a relay point with the real reader, who may or may not "identify" with him—that is, *accept as meant for himself* what the narrator says to his extradiegetic narratee—whereas in no case can the real reader identify (in this sense) with the intradiegetic narratee, who is, after all, a *character* just like all the others. When Des Grieux says to Renoncour, "You were a

---

[1]Susan Suleiman (*Le Roman à thèse* [Paris: Presses Universitaires de France, 1983], p. 197) very correctly proposes to substitute for "ideological function" the more neutral *interpretative function*.

[2]The double status of Renoncour (and of many others of the same type) does not always seem to be clearly understood. It is, however, simple: he is *intradiegetic as the narratee* of Des Grieux and *extradiegetic as the narrator* (fictive author) of the first narrative of *Manon Lescaut*. And he can be both only because he is a *homodiegetic* narrator—that is, present as a character (among others, as the narratee) in the narrative he takes on. Every extra-homodiegetic narrator is intradiegetic as a character and extradiegetic as the narrator. Clear?

witness to that at Pacy. My meeting with you was a happy moment of release granted me by fate . . . ," I, the "real" reader, do not feel myself to be affected by those remarks. Des Grieux speaks to Renoncour (and with good reason) as one character to another character, who receives that speech and intercepts it totally and legitimately, since he is the only one to whom it can be addressed.[3] But when the narrator of *Père Goriot* writes, "As you hold this book in your white hand, lying back in a softly cushioned armchair, and saying to yourself, 'Perhaps this one is amusing,'"[4] I have a right to object (mentally) that my hands are not so white or that my armchair is not so softly cushioned, which means that I legitimately take those remarks as directed at me. And when Tristram asks me to help him carry Mr. Shandy over to the bed, that metalepsis consists precisely of treating an extradiegetic narratee as if he were intradiegetic. It is completely legitimate to distinguish in principle the narratee from the reader, but one must also take into account cases of syncrisis.[5]

In the same way, of course, the extradiegetic narrator merges totally with the author, whom I shall not call "implied," as

---

[3]That is obviously not the case with all the statements addressed to Renoncour. When Des Grieux promises him, "You will come to know Tiberge as my story continues," we can share this expectation with him. In keeping with the principle *he who can do most can do least,* the intradiegetic narratee can unite the strong role of active listener (he meets Des Grieux) with the weaker role of passive listener (passive because he is external to the story: he does not know Tiberge)—a role that is ours, too.

[4][Trans. Marion Ayton Crawford (Harmondsworth: Penguin, 1951), p. 28.]

[5]It is, moreover, significant that in another article—one devoted, this time, to the reader—Prince implicitly gives up the idea of distinguishing the reader from the narratee (extradiegetic, of course) ("Notes on the Text as Reader," in Susan Suleiman and Inge Crosman, eds., *The Reader in the Text* [Princeton: Princeton University Press, 1980]). His reworking of the 1973 article ("Introduction à l'étude du narrataire," *Poétique* 14 [1973], 178–196) in the 1982 book (*Narratology,* pp. 16–26) marks a little more clearly the distinction between the (intradiegetic) "character-narratees" and the others but does not draw all the conclusions from that distinction.

people too often do, but rather entirely explicit and declared. Nor shall I say he is "real"; but he is sometimes (rarely) real, like, let us say, the Giono of *Noé*, recognizable by his dressing gown "cut from a red horse-blanket" and other auto-biographical details; sometimes fictive (Robinson Crusoe); sometimes some odd hybrid of the two, like the narrator-author of *Tom Jones*, who "is" not Fielding but who nonetheless weeps once or twice for his deceased Charlotte. But I want to avoid encroaching on my next chapter, which will attempt to grapple with, or evade head on, this thorny question.

My last reservation bears on another syncrisis not dealt with by Prince, which provides for one of the possible functions of the narratee: this is the identity *between narratee and hero*, and it is the situation called "second-person narrating." That situation is characteristic of certain legal or academic narratives and naturally(?) of literary works like *La Modification* (in the second-person plural) or *Un Homme qui dort* (in the second-person singular); and the term "second-person narrating" seems to me to fully define the situation. This rare but very simple case is a variant of heterodiegetic narrating—proof, at least, that heterodiegetic narrating extends beyond "third-person narrative." By definition, every narrating that is not (that does not have—or pretends not to have—any occasion to be) in the first person is heterodiegetic.[6] But besides *I*, the possibilities are not limited to *he, she,* or *they*; there is also

[6]This obviously includes the case of "second-person autobiography" evoked by Lejeune (*Je est un autre*, p. 36) and admirably exemplified, albeit in verse, by Apollinaire's *Zone*. Making use, as Lejeune remarks, of a very common condition of language (interior dialogue), this type of autobio-heterodiegetic narrative seems less intensely figural or fictive than its third-person version. But it is actually more complex, since it includes the narratee in its action: the character *is* the narratee, he *is not* the narrator, and again, we do not know where the author *pretends to be,* and of course we know or guess that he is everywhere.

you, with [in French] its familiar and formal (singular and plural) variants. This gives me the opportunity to note here that it is wrong to consider persons in the singular only. There are also narratives in the second- or third-person plural, which are still heterodiegetic. And there are narratives in the first-person plural, a case that might seem more complex, since *we = I + he*, or *I + you*, etc.—that is, *ego + aliquis*. Not at all. For a narrative to be homodiegetic, it is enough that *ego* figure in it as a character. For him to figure in it alone would be the absolute form of the autodiegetic. Crusoe before Friday? Thoreau at Walden? Not really. The animal of "The Burrow"? Not enough. Malone? Not yet . . .

19 *Implied Author, Implied Reader?*

Two or three gaps may remain for me to fill or justify, gaps I have occasionally been taken to task for, particularly by Shlomith Rimmon. I say two or three, for one of the three consisted of the lack of correlation among what Rimmon calls "the various aspects of narrative"[1] (tense, mood, voice), and I have just done what I could to make good that omission.

Another concerns the idea of *character* studied in itself. Rimmon attributes that gap to my being exclusively concerned with action as the main object of narrative—from which it follows (according to the Aristotelian way of thinking) that the characters are nothing but *carriers* of the action. That viewpoint has a lot to be said for it. After all, if a character is not caught up in an action, he can hardly appear in a narrative (though he may appear in a portrait, a character sketch, etc.). But I would add that *Narrative Discourse*—more radically and (once again) as its title indicates and its introduction corroborates—bears on narrative *discourse* and not on its *objects*. Now, characters belong in that latter category, even if, in fiction, they are obviously only *pseudo-objects* and, like all the objects of fiction, are wholly constituted by the discourse that claims to describe them and report their actions, thoughts,

[1][Rimmon, "Comprehensive Theory of Narrative," p. 57.]

and words. All the more reason, no doubt, to be more interested in the constituting discourse than in the object constituted—this "living being with no insides," which in this situation (unlike that of the historian or the biographer) is only an effect of the text.[2] I note, moreover, that Shlomith Rimmon herself, after devoting to characters as objects a somewhat interrogative chapter ("Story: Characters"), must indeed return to the subject later, and this time with more assurance, under the heading of discourse ("Text: Characterization").[3] *Characterization* is quite obviously the technique of constituting characters with narrative texts. The study of that technique seems to me the greatest concession narratology, in the strict sense, can make to the consideration of character. But I have no regrets about having refused to make the concession, or rather, from my perspective, having not even thought of making it, for it seems to me that by allowing the study of characterization to have the privilege of shaping, and thereby governing, the analysis of narrative discourse, we make *too much* of a concession to what is only one "effect" among others. In my view it is decidedly, although relatively, preferable (more "narratological") to decompose the study of "characterization" into the study of its constituting devices (which are not all specific to it): denomination, description, focalization, narrative of words or thoughts or both, relation to the narrating situation, etc.

The third "gap" calls for more extended comment. The best way to begin is no doubt to quote Shlomith Rimmon in full:

> The omission (again without explanation) of the "implied author" seems to me unfortunate both in itself and in the resulting

---

[2]See Philippe Hamon, "Pour un statut sémiologique du personnage" (1972), in *Poétique du récit* (Paris: Seuil, 1977), and *Le Personnel du roman* (Geneva: Droz, 1983).

[3]Rimmon, *Narrative Fiction.*

creation of a partly false symmetry between the narrator and the narratee. The partial falsity of the symmetry is confined to the *extradiegetic narrator/narratee*. While the extradiegetic narrator is a voice in the text, the extradiegetic narratee, or implied reader is not any element of the text but a mental construct based on the text as a whole. In fact, the implied reader parallels the implied author—another mental construct on the basis of the text as a whole, strictly separate from the real author, whom Genette rightly excludes from his analysis. Without the implied author it is difficult to analyze the "norms" of the text, especially when they differ from those of the narrator.[4]

This, as we see, is not a casual remark: the ideas are most carefully spelled out and all the i's are dotted. It would be easy enough to respond, no doubt, by excluding from the narratological field not only the real author but also the "implied" author, or more exactly the question (for to me it is one) of his existence. Easy and justifiable: in my opinion, narratology has no need to go beyond the narrative situation, and the two agents "implied author" and "implied reader" are clearly situated in that "beyond." But if the question does not, for me, lie within the province of narratology (moreover, it is by no means specific to narrative, and Rimmon quite rightly speaks here of *text* in general), it obviously lies within the broader province of poetics, and perhaps it would be fitting to conclude by considering it on that frontier, which we have now reached. But we cannot do so without trying to disentangle some threads that are rather snarled, and I beg indulgence in advance for that thankless exercise.

First, I note a point of agreement in that for both of us the

[4]Rimmon, "Comprehensive Theory of Narrative" p. 58 [Genette's emphasis]. To tell the truth, once (p. 220) I use the term "implied author," but without thinking of its implications and immediately identifying it with a real author (Saint-Amant).

intradiegetic narrator and intradiegetic narratee remain outside the discussion. Des Grieux and Renoncour run no risk of interfering with the authorial and "lectorial" agents, from whom they are separated by two other agents, the extradiegetic narrator and his extradiegetic narratee (Renoncour the narrator and his receiver); they are sealed off in their diegetic balloon, where we will leave them. The false symmetry consists, according to Rimmon, of symmetrizing the status of the extradiegetic narrator with the status of the extradiegetic narratee, even though the latter merges with the "implied" reader (whom I prefer to call the *potential* reader, but I hope that those two, at least, constitute no more than one), whereas the former cannot be merged with the implied author. All of that can be represented by a diagram like the following:

$$\text{Extradiegetic narrator} \longrightarrow \text{Extradiegetic narratee}$$
$$\neq \text{Implied author} \qquad\qquad = \text{Implied reader}$$

A second point of agreement, then: the extradiegetic narratee merges with the implied or potential reader. So one agent is excised, to the delight of our master Ockham, and these days such small economies are not to be scorned. The discussion therefore turns on the distinction—which Shlomith Rimmon makes and I did not—between extradiegetic narrator and implied author, and on that alone. (There is perhaps a minor disagreement about the way in which Rimmon sees the extradiegetic narratee in the text: "a mental construct based on the text as a whole." The mental construct seems to me to be based at least as much on a network of pinpointed and localized signs, of which Prince has given some excellent illustrations. We are not dealing, as we are in the case of the narrator, with a *voice*, but with an ear sometimes delineated with precision and in detail.)

Let me recall that the notion of implied author was proposed in English in 1961 by Wayne Booth; the French translation *auteur implicite* was unfortunate, for the adjective tends to harden and hypostatize what in English was only a participle.[5] For Booth, that notion of implied author—constructed in opposition to the idea of real author—is broadly identified with the notion of narrator, and sometimes, moreover, Booth happens to replace "implied author" with "implied *narrator*."[6] At a time when the dissociation between the (real) author and the narrator was not very common, *implied author* served to mark their difference and to distinguish, let us say, Henry Fielding himself from the various enunciators of *Tom Jones, Joseph Andrews,* or *Amelia.* For the most part and for each narrative, that gave a total of *two* agents: the real author and the implied author (that is, the image of the real author as it could be constructed—by the reader, of course—on the basis of the text). Since then, the emphasis has been placed on the activity of the narrator, and if we retain the agent "implied author," that makes *three* agents—whence this "complete" table, different variants of which can be found in Chatman, Bronzwaer, Schmid, Lintvelt, and Hoek:

[Real auth. [Impl. auth. [Narrator [Narrative] Narratee] Impl. rder.] Real rder.]

which is already quite a crowd for one narrative. Help, Ockham!

So the question (in considering only the left side of the table) is this: is the *implied author* a necessary and (therefore) valid agent between the narrator and the real author?

As an actual agent, obviously not: a narrative of fiction is produced fictively by its narrator and actually by its (real) author. No one is toiling away between them, and every type of textual performance can be attributed only to one or the

[5]The French expression even gets back into English in the form *implicit author,* which, to tell the truth, Booth himself uses once or twice.
[6]Wayne C. Booth, "The Self-Conscious Narrator in Comic Fiction before *Tristram Shandy,*" PMLA 67 (1952), 164.

other, depending on the level chosen. For example, the style of *Joseph and His Brothers* can be attributed only (fictively) to the celestial narrator who is supposed naturally to speak in that pseudo-biblical language or to Mr. Thomas Mann, a writer in the German language, winner of a Nobel prize for literature, etc., who makes him speak that way. The style of *L'Etranger* in fiction is the way Meursault expresses himself, and in reality it is the way he is made to express himself by an author whom we have no justification for distinguishing from Mr. Albert Camus, a writer in the French language, etc. No place here for the activity of a third person, no reason to release the real author from his actual responsibilities (ideological, stylistic, technical, and other)—except by falling heavily from formalism into angelism.

Now, as an ideal agent: the implied author is defined by its inventor, Wayne Booth, as well as by one of its detractors, Mieke Bal, as an *image* of the (real) author constructed by the text and perceived as such by the reader.[7] The function of this image seems to be essentially ideological in nature. For Shlomith Rimmon, as we have seen, it (alone) allows us to analyze the "norms" of the text; for Mieke Bal, "this notion . . . was very popular because it promised something which, in my view, it has not been able to deliver: it promised to account for the ideology of the text. This would have made it possible to condemn a text without condemning its author and vice versa—a very attractive proposition to the autonomists of the '60s."[8]

---

[7]Booth: "An implicit *picture* of the author who stands behind the scenes" ("Distance and Point of View," *Essays in Criticism* 11 [1961], 64); Bal: "The implied author . . . is the *image* of the overall subject" ("Laughing Mice," p. 209). In her article, Mieke Bal maintains against Bronzwaer (and not unreasonably) that the idea of implied author is incompatible with the type of narratology I propose, particularly with the opposition between intra- and extradiegetic.

[8]Bal, "Notes on Narrative Embedding," p. 42. Readers will have noted in passing that the essential gesture of ideological analysis seems to consist of condemning a text.

We will come back to this aspect of the question. Right now, I propose accepting the definition of implied author as an image of the author in the text. It seems to me to correspond to my experience of reading. I read, for example, *Joseph and His Brothers*; I hear in the text a voice, the voice of the fictive narrator; something(?) tells me that that voice is not Thomas Mann's; and behind the explicit image of that artless and devout narrator I construct as well as I can—and if possible without taking advantage of too many extratextual pieces of information—the image (implied by that fiction) of the author, whom I suppose *a contrario* to be clear-headed and a "free thinker." It is the author as I infer him from his text, it is the image that that text suggests to me of its author.

Logically speaking (back to logic again), an image has no features that are distinct (from those of its model) and thus deserves no special mention, unless it is unfaithful—that is, incorrect. The correctness of the "implied author" image can turn on (only) two factors, connected to its production and its reception. (I am going to become very schematic.) One is the competence of the reader. It goes without saying that an incompetent or stupid reader can, on the basis of the text, construct the most unfaithful image of the author, believing, for example, that Albert Camus was a haggard and inarticulate creature or that Daniel Defoe spent twenty-eight years on a desert island.[9] To eliminate these secondary distortions, we must therefore (by methodological decision) presume the reader to be fully competent. That does not necessarily mean (let us feel reassured) superhuman intelligence, but a minimum of ordinary perspicuity and a good mastery of the codes involved, including, of course, language. *Good* mastery signifies at least, I think, the mastery the author presumes and

[9]"Despite established opinion, many people even today make themselves ridiculous by associating an author with the feelings he attributes to his characters; and if he makes use of the *I*, almost all those people are tempted to confuse him with the narrator" (Balzac, preface to *Le Lys dans la vallée*).

Implied Author, Implied Reader?

counts on; see, for example, the functioning of a classical detective story.

The other factor on which the correctness of the "implied author" image can turn and the only one still a matter of concern to us is the performance of the (real) author, and our question then becomes: in what circumstances can an author produce, in his text, an unfaithful image of himself?

According to the defenders of the implied author themselves, those circumstances can be of two kinds. The first hypothesis is that of the *involuntary revelation* (in the sense in which psychoanalysis speaks of "tell-tale" slips) *of a subconscious personality.* Two arguments are invoked here:[10] one is the testimony of Proust, who asserts, as we all know, "A book is the product of a different *self* [a "second self," Booth would say] from the self we manifest in our habits, in our social life, in our vices. . . ."[11] The other is the famous "Marxist" analysis (anticipated as early as 1870 by Zola) according to which Balzac in the *Comédie humaine* illustrated, without intending to, political and social opinions contrary to those he professed in his lifetime. This is how Lukács, quoted by Lintvelt, set forth that argument in 1951:

> Engels showed that Balzac, although his political creed was legitimist royalism, nevertheless inexorably exposed the vices and weaknesses of royalist feudal France and described its death agony with magnificent poetic vigor. . . . That contradiction in Balzac, a legitimist, reaches its culmination in the fact that of all the characters his world abounds in, the only authentic and true heroes are the ones who resolutely struggle against feudalism and capitalism: the Jacobins and the martyrs of the fighting on the barricades.[12]

[10]For the most part, I follow Lintvelt's argumentation (*Essai*, pp. 18–22).
[11][Marcel Proust, "The Method of Sainte-Beuve," in *Marcel Proust on Art and Literature, 1896–1919*, trans. Sylvia Townsend Warner (New York: Meridian Books, 1958), pp. 99–100.]
[12]Georg Lukács, *Balzac und der französische Realismus* (1952), French translation published by Maspero (1967), pp. 14 and 17, and cited by Lintvelt, *Essai*,

Implied Author, Implied Reader?

That formulation is hardly the most discriminating and shrewdest one imaginable,[13] but never mind: Balzac had no trouble appearing less of a conservative in his work than in his manifestos, the ideological contradiction and what Engels calls the "triumph of realism" possibly form a less Epinalian pattern,[14] and in any case, here the quickest way to proceed is by assuming the validity of the example. What conclusions can we draw in the two cases (Proust and Balzac) and in all the cases dealt with daily by psychocriticism and sociocriticism? Obviously, that the image of the author constructed by the (competent) reader is *more faithful* than the idea that that author had of himself; Proust, moreover, is speaking here of a "deep self" that must indeed be *more true* than the "superficial" self of consciousness. Here, therefore, *the implied author is the* authentic *real author*. To play the scientist, we will write IA = RA. In this case, of course, IA—a faithful and thus transparent image—becomes an unnecessary agent. Exit IA.

p. 20. [The English translation of the first sentence is from Lukács, "Preface," *Studies in European Realism* (New York: Grosset & Dunlap, 1964), p. 10; the English translation of the second sentence, which does not appear in that preface, is my translation of the French translation.]

[13]Unfortunately it cannot be attributed to the combination of circumstances existing in the year 1951, the date of this preface and a bad year [for vineyards] if there ever was one. The argument already exists in the texts composed in the 1930s and comes straight from Engels himself, for whom "the only men of whom [Balzac] always speaks with undisguised admiration, are his bitterest political antagonists, the republican heroes of the Cloître Saint Merri, the men, who at that time (1830–36) were indeed the representatives of the popular masses" (draft letter of April 1888, in "The Problem of Realism," *Marx and Engels on Literature and Art*, ed. Lee Baxandall and Stefan Morawski [St. Louis and Milwaukee: Telos Press, 1973]). In question, obviously, is Michel Chrestien of *Illusions perdues* and *Cadignan*, about whom d'Arthez declares, "Among the heroes of Antiquity I know of no man superior to him." To leap from that to the conclusion that *Balzac* admired him more than any other of his heroes . . . see note 9 above. And why should a Legitimist necessarily—under the July monarchy—consider the republicans his "bitterest political antagonists"?

[14][The expression "l'imagerie d'Epinal" refers to drawings that are very precise and detailed but also a little unsophisticated and idealized in the impressions they give of their subjects.]

143

The second hypothesis is that of the deliberate simulation, by the real author and in his work, of a personality different from his real personality or from the idea he has of it (here, as a hypothesis and to avoid taking unnecessary detours, let us suppose his idea to be accurate).

Here, of course, we must isolate and disregard the case of narratives with clearly distinct and, as Booth says, "dramatized" homodiegetic narrators, like *Tristram Shandy*, the *Recherche*, and *Doctor Faustus*. In those books all the effort of simulation bears on the figure of the narrator; the image of the author is in no way affected by it, and only the incompetent reader evoked by Balzac, and perhaps illustrated by Engels, could assimilate Sterne to Tristram or Mann to Zeitblom (with the *Recherche*, as we know, the matter is more complex). Here there is an explicit fictive-author-extradiegetic-homodiegetic-narrator (Tristram), and behind him an implied author who has no reason—and, I will add, no way—to distinguish himself from the real author. So here, too, IA = RA, and exit IA. The case of heterodiegetic narrators is more delicate and more interesting, since there we have an anonymous, and thus (more) implicit, author-narrator, whose personality[15] can in reality be (deliberately) distinct, indeed (generally) ironic: for example, the cheery and self-satisfied narrator of *Tom Jones*, the "middle-of-the-road" narrator of *Leuwen*, or the devout narrator of *Joseph*. These ironies, like all ironies, are produced to be decoded, if not by everyone, at least by the "happy few," on pain of being a wasted effort:

[15]I say *personality* and not *identity*. In principle, the identity of an extra-heterodiegetic narrator is simply not mentioned, and nothing compels (and consequently, nothing authorizes) us to distinguish it from the identity of the author; after all, when the narrator of *Joseph Andrews* makes a reference to his "friend Hogarth" and the narrator of *Tom Jones* makes one or two references to his deceased Charlotte, he is indeed signing himself Henry Fielding. The narrator, therefore, is Fielding himself, but pretending in part to a personality that is not his own.

one does not laugh very well all alone. So we have here two implied agents, but one is the extradiegetic narrator, the other is the image of the author that the reader extracts from the text by decoding the irony, and I see no reason for this image to be unfaithful. Here again, IA = RA, and exit IA.

So IA seems to me, *in general,* to be an imaginary ("residual," says Mieke Bal) agent constituted by two distinctions that remain blind to each other: (1) IA is not the narrator, (2) IA is not the real author, and it is never seen that the first is a matter of the real author and the second is a matter of the narrator, with no room anywhere for a third agent that would be *neither* the narrator *nor* the real author.

I will not, however, claim that this principle brooks no exception—that is, that there is no situation in which the image of the author held up by the text may not be constitutionally unfaithful. Determined to be the self-appointed devil's advocate, I have conscientiously sought some examples of it, and at first I thought I found several in the realm of what I call hypertextuality,[16] where a work signed by a single author arises in fact from the unintentional collaboration of one or several others. On being put to the test, hypertextuality does not seem to me enough to produce an inaccurate authorial image. In reality, in the great majority of cases the hypertextual situation is clearly signaled, and the reader, helped or not by paratextual markers, is in any case *entrusted* by the generic contract with responsibility for perceiving the (inter)authorial relation accurately. Thus, in a parody the reader must identify the parodied text, and therefore its author, behind the parodying text. The reader of *Le Chapelain décoiffé* must recognize both the hypotext *Le Cid,* and therefore the hypotextual author Corneille, and its parodic transformation, and therefore a parodist, whether identified or

[16]See *Palimpsestes,* passim.

not. The reader of *Virgile travesti* must perceive both Virgil and his parodist; the optimal reader of *Vendredi* must recognize Defoe beneath Tournier, etc.[17] Likewise, the reader of a pastiche must identify the author on whom it is modeled (in general, the pasticher helps with that) and must therefore perceive in the pastiche the double presence of the pasticher and the pastiched. So in all these cases the doubleness of the authorial agent is in principle clearly perceived by the reader, and the double "implied author" corresponds entirely to the double real author. So here, too, IA = RA, exit IA.

The exception here seems to me limited to two situations, both of which, furthermore, are fraudulent—that is, constructed precisely in such a way as to deceive the reader by holding up for him, with no corrective sign, an unfaithful image of the author. One of these situations is that of an *apocryphal* work, a perfect imitation without a tell-tale paratext. The reader of an apocryphal work is obviously not supposed to identify in it the doubleness of its authorial agent. In a perfect false-Rimbaud, he is supposed to perceive one author and one only—Rimbaud, of course. The text contains an implied author. Let us speak more plainly: the text implies an author—who is Rimbaud; but the real author is (for example) John Doe. So here, at last, IA ≠ RA.

The other fraudulent situation is the symmetrical one that everyday language, in French, decks out in a somewhat racist term.[18] When a celebrity of the stage or the political scene

---

[17]In this latter case I add "*optimal* reader" because certainly Tournier's performance, richer in itself, dispenses more easily than Boileau's or Scarron's with an identification of the hypotext: there are degrees in the strength of the hypertextual connection. But I maintain that even here the hypertextual reading is *superior* (and, incidentally, more in keeping with the author's intention and therefore with the plan of the text) to a naive reading that is unaware of one aspect of the text.

[18][The French equivalent of "ghostwriter" is "nègre."]

puts his own name to a book written by an anonymous piece-worker in exchange for payment, again the reader is not supposed to perceive the two authorial agents. He perceives one of them, which is not the real one. So here, again, IA ≠ RA.

That is all at the moment, and it is not much, I agree, and it is predictably peripheral. It is even less than that, for the second case is not supposed to exist (thus, as will have been noted, I cited no example), and the first exists only ideally. I know of no apocryphal work that is really perfect and definitively successful.[19] But there exists at least yet a third case of the dissociation of agents: that of works written in collaboration, like the novels of the brothers Goncourt or Tharaud, of Erckmann-Chatrian, or of Boileau-Narcejac.[20] I find it hard to imagine that the *texts* of these works indicate or betray the dualness of their authorial agents. A reader not provided with the paratextual indication of the name of the authors would thus spontaneously construct the image of a single author,[21] and here again IA ≠ RA. This case is not particularly thrilling, but it has the merit of legality. I definitely see no other cases, but it's open season.

My position on the "implied author," then, in one sense remains basically negative. But in another sense I would

[19]Stupid: by definition, if one exists, nobody knows about it.

[20]One must exclude from this class the nonfictional (which in French are the autobiographical) homodiegetic narratives, like the *Journal* of those same Goncourts, in which the authorial dualness is immediately implied by the actorial dualness: *we.*

[21]However, the paratextual indication may be equivocal (as in "Erckmann-Chatrian" or "Boileau-Narcejac," which might be taken for an individual double-name) or it may be false (as in "Delly" or "Ellery Queen," whose real double identity I suppose few readers are aware of, and those few only by an avowedly extratextual means). For Delly, the two real authors—Marie and Frédéric Petitjean de la Rosière—carried the dissimulation of their identity so far as to dedicate their first book (*Une Femme supérieure*, 1907) "to *my* dear parents," which injects the pseudonymous fiction where, in principle, it does not belong. Fortunately, however, they were brother and sister . . .

147

readily call it basically positive. Indeed, everything depends on the status one wants to assign to the notion. If one means by it that beyond the narrator (even an extradiegetic one), and by various pinpointed or global signs, the narrative text (like any other text) produces a certain *idea* (taking everything into account, this term is preferable to "image," and it is high time to substitute it for image) *of the author*, one means something obvious, which I can only acknowledge and even insist on, and *in this sense* I willingly approve of Bronzwaer's formula: "The scope of narrative theory [I would say, more carefully, of poetics] excludes the writer but includes the implied author."[22] The implied author is everything the text lets us know about the author, and the literary theorist, like every other reader, must not disregard it. But if one wants to establish this *idea of the author* as a "narrative agent," I don't go along, maintaining always that agents should not be multiplied unnecessarily—and this one, *as such*, seems to me unnecessary. In narrative, or rather behind or before it, there is someone who tells, and who is the narrator. On the narrator's far side there is someone who writes, who is responsible for everything on the near side. That someone—big news—is the author (and no one else), and it seems to me, as Plato said some time ago, that that is enough.

I would indeed say as much—that is, as little—in the matter of the reader. A reader is more or less implied in the text, and in extradiegetic narrating that implied reader merges with the narratee and consists wholly of the signs that imply and sometimes designate him. In intradiegetic narrating, the implied reader is masked by the narratee and can be alluded to by no pinpointed sign; Des Grieux can address no one *beyond* Renoncour. But in fact he remains comprehensively

[22]W. J. M. Bronzwaer, "Implied Author, Extradiegetic Narrator, and Public Reader: G. Genette's Narratological Model and the Reading Version of *Great Expectations*," *Neophilologus* 62 (1978), 3.

implied by the competence—linguistic and narrative, among other kinds—that the text postulates in expecting to be read: Des Grieux speaks only to Renoncour, but Renoncour awaits a reader.

The great dissymmetry in all of that is due to the *vectorality* of narrative communication. The author of a narrative, like every author, addresses a reader who does not yet exist at the moment the author is addressing him, and who may never exist.[23] Contrary to the implied author, who is the idea, in the reader's head, of a real author, the implied reader is the idea, in the real author's head, of a *possible* reader. Bronzwaer is therefore right to dispute my claim that Renoncour, "although fictive, . . . addresses the actual public, just like Rousseau or Michelet."[24] Not for the reason he gives—that a fictive person cannot address a real public—but because no author, not even Rousseau or Michelet, can address in writing a real reader: every author can address only a possible reader. Furthermore, even a letter does not address a real and definite recipient unless we *assume* that that recipient reads it; but he can *at least* die beforehand, I mean *instead* of receiving it; that happens all the time. Until the recipient reads it (and, therefore, for the scribe in his scriptorium), however definite the recipient may be as a person, he remains potential as a reader. So perhaps it would positively be better to rechristen "implied reader" *potential reader*.[25] Whence the following revision of the overly popular diagram of narrative "agents":

RA (IA) → Narrator → Narrative → Narratee → (PR) RR

---

[23]In this respect the oral narrator is better off, but "better" is wholly relative: the hearer is certainly there (if he were not, there would be no narrating), but are you very sure he is listening?

[24]*Narrative Discourse*, p. 229; Bronzwaer, "Implied Author," p. 7.

[25]On this always potential or "conjectural" nature of the reader and on the sundry ways—varying down through the centuries—in which the author tries to "fictionalize" him, see Father Ong's excellent article (cited above,

My PR means, therefore, *potential reader,* and my IA is intended to mean (but that is not obvious) *inferred author.* The rest of the notation I leave to the hermeneutic competence of my PR.

This discussion with Wayne Booth, or at least with the (to me[26]) excessive use of an idea he put forward, is my occasion for saying a word in response to his critique of *Narrative Discourse.* An awkward occasion, but no other would have been much less so, for his critique is very general and bears on no one chapter in particular. Outlined in the "Afterword" of the second edition of *The Rhetoric of Fiction,* it is developed in an essay published very soon thereafter.[27]

That essay, more than kind in my regard, is, to tell the truth, only one element in a wide-ranging dispute opposing Booth (and, more generally, the group of neo-Aristotelian Chicago critics) to what he calls the *Frague School*(?), or "deconstructionisticalism," or more generally the French "structuralist and post-structuralist" movement. Seen from Savigny-sur-Orge, the urgency of the polemic does not necessarily leap into view. "Deconstructionist" criticism, that typically American product of a certain reading of Derridism, visibly disturbs the sleep of those who see it as threatening to destroy criticism and literature. By contamination, all postwar European criticism, whether of Marxist, Freudian, or structuralist inspiration, is suspected, in their eyes, of sophistry and nihilism. Compared with that dark anarchistic tide,

---

Chapter 11, note 7). Its title alone already constitutes a salutary warning directed at all of us and in all our roles: "The Writer's Audience Is Always a Fiction"—implying, even "off-fiction" and even "off-literature."

[26]To him also, it seems, since today he asserts that, as he reads the commentaries that have been devoted to that idea, he is "increasingly dissatisfied" (*Rhetoric of Fiction,* 2d ed., p. 422).

[27]Booth, *The Rhetoric of Fiction,* 2d ed., pp. 439 and 441; "Rhetorical Critics Old and New: The Case of Gérard Genette," in Laurence Lerner, ed., *Reconstructing Literature* (Totowa, N.J.: Barnes & Noble, 1983), pp. 123–141.

Narrative Discourse seems a haven of sobriety, method, and rationalism, a book, Booth says, where "on almost every page . . . I am learning how literature and criticism *are done*" (p. 129).

It is always nice to hear a compliment, and I have no need to say how honored I am by praise from a critic of Wayne Booth's stature or how much I share certain of his enthusiasms and his annoyances, plus some others. But finally, since every agreement rests in part on a misunderstanding, from the outset the pair "structuralism and post-structuralism" puts me a little on guard: I perceive in the *post-* of *post-structuralism* as it is brandished in the United States an accent of "going beyond" that prevents me from coupling it with *structuralism*. Just as postmodernism is above all (consider architecture) an antimodernist reaction and a flight into a mannered neo-eclecticism, so poststructuralism, if it is something, can scarcely be anything but a repudiation of structuralism—I have not yet understood in favor of what. Unless the "open structuralism" that I happen to recommend may be itself a variety of poststructuralism?

In short, there is indeed somewhere—at least in our divergent evaluations of structuralism—a disagreement between my values and Wayne Booth's, and his reservations in my regard are obviously due to the way *Narrative Discourse* (not to mention its sequel!) resists attempts to annex it to a given position—attempts that Booth himself declares to be hopeless. He is surprised, for example, by my last bow in the "Afterword" to the Barthesian valuing of the "writerly" or by my own valuing of the "lack of unity" of the *Recherche*. He is irritated at seeing me uphold against Proust the formalist paradox that "vision can also be a matter of style and of technique"—a parodic reversal that is, nonetheless, very restrained. Above, I specified the several avant-garde prejudices I relinquish today, but I will not go so far as to join the ranks of those who psychologize and moralize.

Booth's main reproach is, as a matter of fact, of that kind. *Narrative Discourse*, he says, does indeed show *how* the Proustian narrative *is done*, but it fails to say *what the purpose is*, what the function is of each of the techniques I isolate and define: another instance, then, of the functionalist reproach to which I have already, in this very book, had occasion to respond. Once again, I am not sure that each feature has a precisely assignable function, but especially and more specifically, I cannot—in dealing with the *Recherche*—enter into the perspective of reading that governs Booth's functionalism. For him, indeed, my reading of the *Recherche* is too intellectualist and "scientific," too focused on the notion of narrative *information* and *signification* and (as regards the reader) on the simple sense of intellectual curiosity, to the exclusion of all "moral and emotional entanglement with characters" (p. 127), and especially with the Narrator. He holds that I do not try hard enough to find out how the Proustian narrative mode serves to enlarge our "sympathy" with or our "antipathy" toward those whom we must indeed see, "despite the quiet, unmelodramatic tone [of this narrative, as] heroes and villains" (p. 138).

I have, in fact, a great deal of difficulty applying this Manichaean criterion to the *Recherche*. Not that Proust invested his work with no axiological system but rather, undoubtedly, because he invested it with several (moral, social, aesthetic) that do not all value the same characters or the same groups, so that in my view it would be impossible to designate the "good" and the "bad" in this microcosm that is, after all, unstable and kaleidoscopic, subject to endless reversals. As for the "hero," I do not think I am being false to Proust's intentions in saying that, as the subject of an experience almost continually negative and sometimes laughable until a final revelation of a typically intellectual kind, he inspires in me only very lukewarm feelings. But undoubtedly that is not the main point, and what I have to say about the matter would hold good also for a work with a more unequivocal axiology, like Stendhal's—for I by no means deny that such works exist and are among the greatest and that one of the mechanisms of their functioning is the play, in the reader, of selective identifications, of sympathies and antipathies, of hopes and fears, or, as our common ancestor said, of terror and pity. But I do not believe that the techniques of narrative discourse are especially instrumental in producing these affective impulses. Sympathy or antipathy for a character depends essentially on the psychological or moral (or physical!) characteristics the author gives him, the behavior and speeches he attributes to him, and very little on the techniques of the narrative in which he appears. The aforementioned ancestor noted that the story of Oedipus is as moving when recounted as when represented on the stage, because what makes it so is the action itself; I add only that it is equally moving whatever the (faithful) way in which it is recounted. No doubt I exaggerate, and unquestionably I paid too little attention to these psychological effects, but in returning to them today at Booth's instigation, I see hardly anything but the workings of focalization that can effectually contribute to them. Oriane or Saint-Loup no doubt gain much in being seen through the naive eye of the young Narrator, and Odette or Albertine lose just as much in being spied upon by lovers who are jealous and, as Swann himself says, "neuropathic." I mentioned this, moreover, in *Narrative Discourse*, but I am not sure that those effects do not sometimes turn against their function: the reader is not stupid enough to "adopt" without reservation "points of view" that are so manifestly partial and, further, explicitly given as such. More generally, no doubt, the narrative subtleties of the modern novel (since Flaubert and James)—for example, free indirect style, interior monologue, or multiple focalization—have negative effects, instead, on the reader's desire to approve and no doubt help throw him off the scent, leading "evaluations" astray and discouraging sympathies and antipathies.

To repeat it one last time, *Narrative Discourse* bears on the narrative and the narrating, not on the story, and the strengths and weaknesses, the graces or disgraces of heroes basically depend on neither the narrative nor the narrating but on the story—that is, the content or (and for once this word has to be used) the *diegesis*. To reproach *Narrative Discourse* for disregarding them is to reproach it for its choice of subject. I can, moreover, well enough imagine such a criticism: why do you speak to me of forms, when only content interests me? But if the question is legitimate, the answer is only too obvious: everyone busies himself with whatever arouses his interest, and if the formalists were not here to study forms, who would do it in their place? There will always be enough psychologists to psychologize, ideologues to ideologize, and moralists to moralize, so let us leave the aesthetes to their aesthetics and not expect them to provide results they cannot give. There is a proverb on that subject, and no doubt more than one.

I return briefly to the "implied" author. That ghostly double reminds me, I don't know why, of a story by George Bernard Shaw, or perhaps Oscar Wilde, more or less recast by Mark Twain: everyone knows that the works of Shakespeare were written not by Shakespeare but by one of his contemporaries, who was, moreover, also named Shakespeare. The circumstances of that substitution are less familiar, and here they are. Shakespeare had a twin brother. One day when they were being bathed in the same tub, one of the two slipped and drowned. Since they were absolutely indistinguishable, it was never known which of the two wrote *Hamlet* and which was thrown out with the bath water. The same one, perhaps?

20 *Afterword*

I am not especially inclined to comment on an "afterword" that was itself already a retrospective postscript. Narcissism has its limits, at least technically, and I have trouble seeing myself at the third degree glossing myself glossing. Besides, here and there I have already said what I thought about the motives, implicit elsewhere, that were made explicit there and that I continue basically to accept, with two (or rather one and one-half) exceptions, to which, therefore, I return with a (last) word.

The first bears on my rejection of a "synthesis" (p. 266) of the several categories of tense, mood, and voice—a rejection I justified as a refusal to unify Proust's work artificially. I still feel as much repugnance toward those impositions of "coherence" that interpretative criticism carries off so glibly. And I believe that the more and more faithful (that is, more and more imperfect) condition of the text of the *Recherche* given us today by genetic study tends more and more to deconstruct and destabilize that text's image as a closed and homogeneous work. The Proustian text continuously unravels before our eyes, and the function of narratology is not to recompose what textology decomposes. But as Shlomith Rimmon clearly noted,[1] my rejection of an improper syn-

[1]Rimmon, "Comprehensive Theory of Narrative," p. 57.

thesis served me a little too well as a pretext for shrinking from the requisite task of correlating the constitutive parameters (in Proust or elsewhere) of the various narrative situations. To have these categories intersect in a comprehensive table a priori is not to prejudice or do violence to their capacities for coming together. I have tried to fill that gap by indicating the way such an operation could be carried out, but without bringing it to a conclusion (without giving a complete table of all the possible intersections), because such a completion, aside from being ridiculous and materially impossible, would undoubtedly be more sterilizing than stimulating: a grid should *always* remain open.[2]

The second reservation bears on my valuing the innovative or "subversive" aspects of a work, Proust's or any other. I repudiated above the simplistic conception of the history of art, perhaps simply of History, that such a position implied, but I see that the disavowal was half sketched in on pages 265–266, where I recognized the "unsophisticated" and "romantic" nature of that conception. So all I would have to do is complete the sketch, but that is easier said than done, for I still feel very close—and not from posthumous devotion—to the Barthesian valuing of the "writerly," which I invoked at that time. Today I would simply give it a slightly different meaning, one that obviously commits no one but myself. I would contrast the "writerly" with the "readerly" no longer as the modern to the classical or the deviant to the canonical but, rather, as the potential to the real, as a possibility not yet produced, the theoretical approach to which has the power to indicate its place (the famous empty slot) and its nature. The

[2]"It does not much matter that the table is incomplete," says Philippe Lejeune apropos of another one; "the advantage of a table is that it simplifies, it dramatizes a problem. It should be inspiring. If it were more complicated it would be more accurate but so confusing as to be useless" (Lejeune, "Le Pacte autobiographique [bis]," p. 23).

"writerly" is not only something *already written*, in the rewriting of which the reading plays a role and to which it contributes by its very reading; the "writerly" is also something new, something *unwritten*, whose potentiality is discovered and called attention to by (among others) poetics, through the general nature of its investigation—and whose potentiality poetics invites us to actualize. Who this "us" is and whether the invitation is addressed only to the reader or whether the literary theorist must himself go into action, I am not well equipped to say, or whether the invitation must remain an invitation, a desire unfulfilled, a suggestion without effect— but not always without influence. What is certain is that poetics in general, and narratology in particular, must not limit itself to *accounting for* existing forms or themes. It must also explore the field of what is possible or even *impossible* without pausing too long at that frontier, the mapping out of which is not its job. Until now, critics have done no more than interpret literature. Transforming it is now the task at hand. That is certainly not the business of theoreticians alone; their role is no doubt negligible. Still, what would theory be worth if it were not also good for *inventing practice?*

Bibliography

What follows is a very selective bibliography of narratological studies since 1972, plus some titles that ought to have been included in the bibliography of *Narrative Discourse*. Although selective, this list is probably incomplete (and as of now it is outdated, since no entries were made after June 27, 1983).

Authier, J. "Les Formes du discours rapporté." *Documentation et recherche en linguistique allemande* 17 (1978).

Bachellier, Jean-Louis. "La Poétique lézardée." *Littérature* 12 (December 1973).

Backus, Joseph M. "'He Came into Her Line of Vision Walking Backward': Nonsequential Sequence-Signals in Short Story Openings." *Language Learning* 15 (1965), 67–83.

Bakhtin, Mikhaïl (V. N. Volochinov). "Discours indirect libre en français, en allemand, et en russe." *Le Marxisme et la philosophie du langage.* 1929. Rpt. Paris: Minuit, 1979.

Bal, Mieke. *Narratologie.* Paris: Klincksieck, 1977. (Tr. [chapter 1] "The Narrating and the Focalizing: A Theory of the Agents in Narrative." Trans. Jane E. Lewin. *Style* 17 [1983], 234–269.)

____. *De theorie van vertellen en verhalen: Inleiding in de narratologie.* Muiderberg: Coutinho, 1978.

____. "Notes on Narrative Embedding." *Poetics Today* 2 (1981), 41–59.

____. "The Laughing Mice, or: On Focalization." *Poetics Today* 2 (1981), 202–210.

Bally, Charles. "Le Style indirect libre en français moderne." *Germanisch-Romanische Monatsschrift* 4 (1912).

——. "Figures de pensée et formes linguistiques." *Germanisch-Romanische Monatsschrift* 6 (1914).

Banfield, Ann. "Narrative Style and the Grammar of Direct and Indirect Speech." *Foundations of Language* 10 (1973).

——. "The Formal Coherence of Represented Speech and Thought." *PTL* 3 (1978).

——. "Where Epistemology, Style, and Grammar Meet Literary History: The Development of Represented Speech and Thought." *New Literary History* 9 (1978).

——. "Reflective and Non-Reflective Consciousness in the Language of Fiction." *Poetics Today* 2:2 (Winter 1981).

——. *Unspeakable Sentences: Narration and Representation in the Language of Fiction.* Boston and London: Routledge & Kegan Paul, 1982.

Bann, Stephen. Review of *Narrative Discourse. London Review of Books* (October 1980).

Barth, John. "Tales within Tales within Tales." *Antaeus* 43 (Autumn 1981), 45–63.

Barthes, Roland. "Introduction à l'analyse structurale des récits." *Communications* 8 (1966), 1–27. Reprinted in *Poétique du récit.* Paris: Seuil, 1977. (Tr. "Introduction to the Structural Analysis of Narratives." In *Image—Music—Text.* Trans. Stephen Heath. New York: Hill & Wang, 1977.)

——. "L'Effet de réel." *Communications* 11 (1968), 84–89. *Littérature et réalité.* Paris: Seuil, 1982. (Tr. "The Reality Effect." In Tzvetan Todorov, ed. *French Literary Theory Today: A Reader.* Trans. R. Carter. Cambridge: Cambridge University Press, 1982.)

——. "To Write: An Intransitive Verb?" In *The Languages of Criticism and the Sciences of Man,* ed. Richard Macksey and Eugenio Donato. Baltimore: Johns Hopkins University Press, 1970.

——. "Analyse textuelle d'un conte d'Edgar Poe." In Claude Chabrol et al. *Sémiotique narrative et textuelle.* Paris: Larousse, 1973.

Beach, Joseph Warren. *The Method of Henry James.* New Haven: Yale University Press, 1918.

——. *The Twentieth-Century Novel: Studies in Technique.* New York: Appleton-Century-Crofts, 1932.

Berendsen, Marjet. "The Teller and the Observer: G. Genette's and M. Bal's Theories on Narration and Focalization Examined." Unpublished paper, Hertogenbosch, 1979.

Bickerton, Derek. "Modes of Interior Monologue: A Formal Definition." *Modern Language Quarterly* 28 (1967).

———. "J. Joyce and the Development of Interior Monologue." *Essays in Criticism* 18:1 (1968).

Birge-Vitz, Evelyne. "Narrative Analysis of Medieval Texts." *Modern Language Notes* 92 (1977).

Bonnycastle, S., and A. Kohn. "G. Genette and S. Chatman on Narrative." *Journal of Practical Structuralism* 2 (1980).

Bony, Alain. "La Notion de *persona* ou d'*auteur implicite*: Problèmes d'ironie narrative." *L'Ironie, linguistique et sémiologie* 2. Lyons: Presses Universitaires de Lyon, 1978.

Booth, Wayne C. "The Self-Conscious Narrator in Comic Fiction before *Tristram Shandy*." *PMLA* 67 (1952), 163–185.

———. "Distance and Point of View." *Essays in Criticism* 11 (1961), 60–79. (Tr. "Distance et point de vue." In *Poétique du récit*. Paris: Seuil, 1977.)

———. *The Rhetoric of Fiction*. 2d ed. Chicago: University of Chicago Press, 1983.

———. "Rhetorical Critics Old and New: The Case of Gérard Genette." In *Reconstructing Literature*, ed. Laurence Lerner. Totawa, N.J.: Barnes & Noble, 1983.

Bronzwaer, W. J. M. *Tense in the Novel*. Groningen: Wolters-Noordhoff, 1970.

———. "Implied Author, Extradiegetic Narrator, and Public Reader: G. Genette's Narratological Model and the Reading Version of *Great Expectations*." *Neophilologus* 62 (1978).

———. "M. Bal's Concept of Focalization." *Poetics Today* 2 (1981), 193–201.

Brooke-Rose, Christine. *A Rhetoric of the Unreal*. Cambridge: Cambridge University Press, 1981.

Bruss, Elizabeth. *Autobiographical Acts*. Baltimore: Johns Hopkins University Press, 1977.

Charles, Michel. *Rhétorique de la lecture*. Paris: Seuil, 1977.

Chatelain, Danièle. "Itération interne et scène classique." *Poétique* 51 (1982), 369–381.

Bibliography

Chatman, Seymour. *Story and Discourse: Narrative Structure in Fiction and Film.* Ithaca: Cornell University Press, 1978.

——. Review of *Narrative Discourse. Journal of Aesthetics and Art Criticism* 39 (Winter 1980).

Cohn, Dorrit. "Narrated Monologue: Definition of a Fictional Style." *Comparative Literature* 18 (1966).

——. "K. Enters *The Castle:* On the Change of Person in Kafka's Manuscript." *Euphorion* 62 (1968).

——. *Transparent Minds: Narrative Modes for Presenting Consciousness in Fiction.* Princeton: Princeton University Press, 1978. (Tr. *La Transparence intérieure.* Trans. Alain Bony. Paris: Seuil, 1981.)

——. "The Encirclement of Narrative." *Poetics Today* 2:2 (Winter 1981), 157–182.

Crosman, Inge. *Metaphoric Narration.* Chapel Hill: University of North Carolina Press, 1978.

Culler, Jonathan. *Structuralist Poetics.* Ithaca: Cornell University Press, 1975.

——. "Foreword" to Gérard Genette, *Narrative Discourse.* Translation of "Discours du récit," a portion of *Figures III.* Trans. Jane E. Lewin. Ithaca: Cornell University Press, 1980.

Dällenbach, Lucien. *Le Récit spéculaire.* Paris: Seuil, 1977.

Danon-Boileau, Laurent. *Produire le fictif.* Paris: Klincksieck, 1982.

Debray-Genette, Raymonde. "La Pierre descriptive." *Poétique* 43 (1980), 293–304.

——. "Traversées de l'espace descriptif." *Poétique* 51 (1982), 329–344.

Demoris, René. *Le Roman à la première personne.* Paris: Colin, 1975.

Dillon, G. L., and F. Kirchoff. "On the Form and Function of Free Indirect Style." *PTL* 1:3 (1976).

Doležel, Lubomir. "The Typology of the Narrator: Point of View in Fiction." *To Honor R. Jakobson.* Mouton, 1967.

——. *Narrative Modes in Czech Literature.* Toronto: University of Toronto Press, 1973.

Fitch, Brian T. *Narrateur et narration dans "l'Etranger" d'Albert Camus.* Paris: Minard, 1960.

Friedemann, Käte. *Die Rolle des Erzählers in der Epik.* Leipzig, 1910.

Friedman, Norman. *Form and Meaning in Fiction.* Athens: University of Georgia Press, 1975 (chapter 8, a revised version of "Point of View in Fiction," *PMLA* 70 [1955]).

Genette, Gérard. *Figures III*. Paris: Seuil, 1972.

____. *Introduction à l'architexte*. Paris: Seuil, 1979.

____. *Narrative Discourse*. Translation of "Discours du récit," a portion of *Figures III*. Trans. Jane E. Lewin. Ithaca: Cornell University Press, 1980.

____. *Palimpsestes: La Littérature au second degré*. Paris: Seuil, 1982.

Glowinski, Michal. "Der Dialog im Roman." *Poetica* 8 (1976).

____. "On the First-Person Novel." *New Literary History* 9:1 (Fall 1977).

Gothot-Mersch, Claudine. "La Parole des personnages" (1981). *Travail de Flaubert*. Paris: Seuil, 1983.

Guiraud, Pierre. "Modern Linguistics Looks at Rhetoric: Free Indirect Style." In *Patterns of Literary Style*, ed. Joseph Strelka. University Park: Penn State University Press, 1971.

Hamburger, Käte. *Die Logik der Dichtung*. Stuttgart: Ernst Klett, 1957. (Tr. *The Logic of Literature*. Trans. Marilynn J. Rose. 2d rev. ed. Bloomington: Indiana University Press, 1973.)

Hamon, Philippe. "Pour un statut sémiologique du personnage" (1972). In *Poétique du récit*. Paris: Seuil, 1977.

____. "Sur quelques concepts narratologiques." *Les Lettres romanes* 33:1 (1979).

____. *Introduction à l'analyse du descriptif*. Paris: Hachette, 1981.

____. *Le Personnel du roman*. Geneva: Droz, 1983.

Harweg, Roland. *Pronomina und Textkonstitution*. Munich: Fink, 1968.

Hayman, David. Review of *Figures III*. *Novel* 6:3 (1973).

Hernadi, Paul. "Dual Perspective: Free Indirect Discourse and Related Techniques." *Comparative Literature* 24 (1972).

Hoek, Leo H. *La Marque du titre: Dispositifs sémiotiques d'une pratique textuelle*. Mouton, 1982.

Holmshawi, Lorraine. "Les Exilés de la narratologie: Quelques remarques sur le rythme et les images dans un extrait de *Madame Bovary*." *French Studies in Southern Africa* 10 (1981), 22–29.

Iser, Wolfgang. *Der Implizit Leser*. Munich: Fink, 1972. (Tr. *The Implied Reader*. Baltimore: Johns Hopkins University Press, 1974.)

____. *Der Akt des Lesens*. Munich: Fink, 1976. (Tr. *The Act of Reading*. Baltimore: Johns Hopkins University Press, 1978.)

Jacquet, Marie-Thérèse. "La Fausse Libération du dialogue ou le 'style direct intégré' dans *Bouvard et Pécuchet*." *Annali della Facolta di Lingue et Letterature straniere dell' Universita di Bari* 1:1 (1980).

Jost, François. "Narration(s): en deçà et au-delà." *Communications* 38 (1983).

———. "Du nouveau roman au nouveau romancier: Questions de narratologie." Thesis, Ecole des Hautes Etudes en Sciences Sociales, Paris, 1983.

Kalepky, Theodor. "Mischung indirekter und direkter Rede . . . ." *Zeitschrift für romanische Philologie* 23 (1889).

Kalik-Teljatnicova, A. "De l'origine du prétendu style indirect libre." *Le Français moderne* 33 (1965–1966).

Kayser, Wolfgang J. "Wer erzählt den Roman?" *Die Vortragsreise.* Bern, 1958. (Tr. "Qui raconte le roman?" In *Poétique du récit.* Paris: Seuil, 1977.)

Kuroda, S. Y. "Where Epistemology, Style, and Grammar Meet." In *A Festschrift for Morris Halle*, ed. Paul Kiparsky. New York: Holt, Rinehart and Winston, 1973. (Tr. "Où l'épistémologie . . . ." *Aux quatre coins de la linguistique.* Paris: Seuil, 1979.)

———. "Reflections on the Foundations of Narrative Theory from a Linguistic Point of View." In *Pragmatics of Language and Literature*, ed. Teun A. van Dijk. Amsterdam: North-Holland; and New York: American Elsevier, 1976. (Tr. "Réflexions sur les fondements de la théorie de la narration." *Langue, discours, société.* Paris: Seuil, 1975.)

Lejeune, Philippe. *Le Pacte autobiographique.* Paris: Seuil, 1975. (Tr. [chapter 1] "The Autobiographical Contract." In Tzvetan Todorov, ed. *French Literary Theory Today: A Reader.* Trans. R. Carter. Cambridge: Cambridge University Press, 1982.)

———. *Je est un autre.* Paris: Seuil, 1980.

———. "Le Pacte autobiographique (bis)." *Actes du IIe colloque international sur l'autobiographie . . . .* Aix-en-Provence: Presses de l'Université de Provence, 1982. (For an expanded version of this article, see *Poétique* 56 [1983], 416–434.)

Lerch, Eugen. "Die stylistische Bedeutung des Imperfekts der Rede." *Germanisch-Romanische Monatsschrift* 6 (1914).

———. "Ursprung und Bedeutung der sog. 'Erlebten Rede.'" *Germanisch-Romanische Monatsschrift* 16 (1928).

Lerch, G. "Die uneigentlich direkte Rede." *Idealistische Philologie.* Heidelberg, 1922.

Liebow, Cynthia. "La Transtextualité dans *The Sot-Weed Factor* de John Barth." Thesis, Ecole des Hautes Etudes en Sciences Sociales, Paris, 1982.

Lintvelt, Jaap. *Essai de typologie narrative: Le Point de vue.* Paris: Corti, 1981.

Lorck, Etienne. *Die erlebte Rede: Eine sprachliche Untersuchung.* Heidelberg, 1921.

Lyotard, Jean-François. "Petite économie libidinale d'un dispositif narratif." *Des dispositifs pulsionnels.* Union Générale d'Editions 10/18, 1973.

McHale, Brian. "Free Indirect Discourse: A Survey of Recent Accounts." *PTL* 3:2 (April 1978).

———. Review of Roy Pascal, *The Dual Voice. PTL* 3:2 (April 1978).

———. "Islands on the Stream of Consciousness." *Poetics Today* 2:2 (1981).

Macksey, Richard, and Eugenio Donato, eds. *The Languages of Criticism and the Sciences of Man.* Baltimore: Johns Hopkins University Press, 1970.

Magny, Claude-Edmonde. *L'Age du roman américain.* Paris: Seuil, 1948.

Molinié, Georges. *Du roman grec au roman baroque.* Toulouse: Université de Toulouse (Le Mirail), 1982.

Mosher, Harold. "The Structuralism of G. Genette." *Poetics* 5:1 (1976).

———. "A Reply to Some Remarks on Genette's Structuralism." *Poetics* 7:3 (1978).

———. "Recent Studies in Narratology." *Papers on Language and Literature* (1981).

Nøjgaard, Morten. Review of *Figures III. Revue Romane* 9:1 (1974).

Ong, Walter J., S.J. "The Writer's Audience Is Always a Fiction." *PMLA* 90 (1975), 9–21.

Orwell, George. "Charles Dickens." (1940). Reprinted in *Selected Essays.* London, 1961.

Pascal, Roy. "Tense and Novel." *Modern Language Review* 57 (1962).

———. *The Dual Voice: Free Indirect Speech and Its Functioning in the Nineteenth-Century European Novel.* Manchester: Manchester University Press, 1977.

Petit, Jacques. "Une Relecture de Mauriac . . . ." *Edition et interprétation des manuscrits littéraires.* Bern, 1981.

Pier, John. "L'Instance narrative du récit à la première personne." Ph.D. diss. New York University, 1983.

——. "Diegesis." In Thomas A. Sebeok et al. *Encyclopedic Dictionary of Semiotics.* Berlin, New York, and Amsterdam: Mouton, 1986. [Genette's bibliography refers to this work as "forthcoming."]

Plénat, M. "Sur la grammaire du style indirect libre." *Cahiers de grammaire* 1. Université de Toulouse (Le Mirail), October 1979.

Pratt, Mary Louise. *Toward a Speech Act Theory of Literary Discourse.* Bloomington: Indiana University Press, 1977.

Prince, Gerald. "Introduction à l'étude du narrataire." *Poétique* 14 (1973), 178–196.

——. *A Grammar of Stories.* The Hague: Mouton, 1973.

——. "Notes on the Text as Reader." In *The Reader in the Text*, ed. Susan Suleiman and Inge Crosman. Princeton: Princeton University Press, 1980.

——. "Reading and Narrative Competence." *L'Esprit créateur* 21:2 (1981).

——. "Narrative Analysis and Narratology." *New Literary History* 13 (1982), 179–188.

——. *Narratology: The Form and Function of Narrative.* The Hague: Mouton, 1982.

Puech, Jean Benoît. "L'Auteur supposé: Essai de typologie des écrivains imaginaires en littérature." Thesis, Ecole des Hautes Etudes en Sciences Sociales, Paris, 1982.

Ricardou, Jean. *Nouveaux Problèmes du roman.* Paris: Seuil, 1978.

Ricoeur, Paul, et al. *La Narrativité.* Ed. du Centre National de Recherche Scientifique, 1980.

Riffaterre, Michael. "L'Illusion référentielle" (1978). *Littérature et réalité.* Paris: Seuil, 1982.

Rimmon, Shlomith. "A Comprehensive Theory of Narrative: G. Genette's *Figures III* and the Structuralist Study of Fiction." *PTL* 1:1 (1976).

——. "Problems of Voice in V. Nabokov's *The Real Life of Sebastian Knight*." *PTL* 1:3 (1976).

——. *Narrative Fiction: Contemporary Poetics.* London: Methuen, 1983.

Ringler, Susan. "Narrators and Narrative Contexts in Fiction." Ph.D. diss., Stanford University, 1981.

Ron, Moshe. "Free Indirect Discourse, Mimetic Language Games, and the Subject of Fiction." *Poetics Today* 2:2 (1981).

Rousset, Jean. *Narcisse romancier: Essai sur la première personne dans le roman.* Paris: Corti, 1973.

Schmid, Wolf. *Der Textaufbau in den Erzählungen Dostoevskys.* Munich: Fink, 1973.

Scholes, Robert. *Structuralism in Literature.* New Haven: Yale University Press, 1974.

———. *Semiotics and Interpretation.* New Haven: Yale University Press, 1982.

Searle, John R. "The Logical Status of Fictional Discourse." *New Literary History* 6:2 (1975).

Sørensen, Kathrine. *La Théorie du roman: Thèmes et modes.* Thesis, Ecole des Hautes Etudes en Sciences Sociales, Paris, 1983. [Sørensen Ravn Jørgensen, Kathrine. *La Théorie du roman: Thèmes et modes.* Copenhagen: Nyt Nordisk Forlag Arnold Busck, 1987.]

Souriau, Etienne. "La Structure de l'univers filmique et le vocabulaire de la filmologie." *Revue internationale de filmologie* 7–8 (1948).

Spielhagen, Friedrich. *Beiträge zur Theorie und Technik des Romans.* Leipzig: L. Staackmann, 1883.

———. *Neue Beiträge zur Theorie und Technik der Epik und Dramatik.* Leipzig, 1898.

Stanzel, Franz K. *Die typischen Erzählsituationen im Roman.* Vienna: Wilhelm Braumüller, 1955. (Tr. *Narrative Situations in the Novel.* Trans. James P. Pusack. Bloomington: Indiana University Press, 1971.)

———. *Typische Formen des Romans.* Göttingen: Vandenhoeck & Ruprecht, 1964.

———. "Second Thoughts on Narrative Situations in the Novel." *Novel* 11 (1978).

———. *Theorie des Erzählens.* Göttingen: Vandenhoeck & Ruprecht, 1979. (Tr. *A Theory of Narrative.* Trans. Charlotte Goedsche. Cambridge: Cambridge University Press, 1984.)

———. "Teller-Characters and Reflector-Characters in Narrative Theory." *Poetics Today* 2 (1981), 5–15.

Sternberg, Meir. *Expositional Modes and Temporal Ordering in Fiction.* Baltimore: Johns Hopkins University Press, 1978.

――. "Proteus in Quotation-Land: Mimesis and the Forms of Reported Discourse." *Poetics Today* 3 (1982), 107–156.

Strauch, G. "De quelques interprétations récentes du style indirect libre." *Recherches anglaises et américaines* (1974).

Suleiman, Susan. Review of *Figures III. French Review* 48 (October 1974).

――. *Le Roman à thèse.* Paris: Presses Universitaires de France, 1983.

Tamir, Nomi. "Some Remarks on a Review of G. Genette's Structuralism." *Poetics* 5:4 (1976).

――. "Personal Narrative and Its Linguistic Foundation." *PTL* 1 (1976), 403–430.

Thibaudet, Albert. *Gustave Flaubert.* Paris: Gallimard, 1935.

Tillotson, Kathleen. *The Tale and the Teller.* London: R. Hart-Davis, 1959.

Tobler, A. "Vermischte Beitrage zur französischen Grammatik." *Zeitschrift für romanische Philologie* 11 (1887).

Todorov, Tzvetan. *Poétique.* Paris: Seuil, 1973 (new version of "Poétique" [1968]). (Tr. *Introduction to Poetics.* Trans. Richard Howard. Minneapolis: University of Minnesota Press, 1981.)

Ullman, Stephen. *Style in the French Novel.* Cambridge: Cambridge University Press, 1957.

Uspenski, Boris. *Poétika Kompozicii.* Moscow, 1970. (Partial French translation: "Poétique de la composition." *Poétique* 9 [1972]. English translation: *A Poetics of Composition.* Trans. Valentina Zavarin and Susan Wittig. Berkeley: University of California Press, 1973.)

Van den Heuvel, Pierre. "Le Discours rapporté." *Neophilologus* 57:1 (1978).

Van Rees, C. J. "Some Issues in the Study of Conceptions of Literature: A Critique of the Instrumentalist View of Literary Theories." *Poetics* 10 (1981), 49–89.

Verschoor, J. A. *Etude de grammaire historique et de style sur le style direct et les styles indirects en français.* Groningen, 1959.

Vitoux, Pierre. "Le Jeu de la focalisation." *Poétique* 51 (1982), 359–368.

Walzel, Oskar. "Von 'Erlebter' Rede." *Zeitschrift für Bucherfreunde.* 1924.

_____. *Das Wortkunstwerk.* Leipzig: Quelle & Meyer, 1926. Rpt. Heidelberg: Quelle & Meyer, 1968.

Weissman, Frida S. "Le Monologue intérieur: A la première, à la deuxième ou à la troisième personne?" *Travaux de linguistique et de littérature* 14:2 (1976).

P.S. (September 2, 1983): I take advantage of a final review of the proofs to call attention to an article that I could not consider in my work but with which I basically agree (it is a critique of Banfield's *Unspeakable Sentences*): Brian McHale, "Unspeakable Sentences, Unnatural Acts," *Poetics Today* 1 (1983).

Index of Authors and Titles

Index of Authors and Titles

Library of Congress Cataloging-in-Publication Data

Genette, Gérard, 1930–
   Narrative discourse revisited.

   Translation of: Nouveau discours du récit.
   Bibliography: p.
   Includes index.
   1. Discourse analysis, Narrative. I. Title.
P320.7.G4613   1988   808'.00141   88-47730
ISBN 0-8014-1758-1 (alk. paper)